More Praise for *What's Your Formula?*

"*As someone who trains groups every day, this book gave me fresh new ways to think about my programs. I especially loved the insights on the radioactive elements of training sessions!*"

> —**Melissa Marshall**, TED Speaker, Founder, Present Your Science

"*Brian Washburn breaks down key training elements in* What's Your Formula? *making it an effective tool for HR professionals. I highly recommend it for anyone responsible for delivering training programs.*"

> —**Michelle Jones**, Chief Human Resources Officer at a
> professional association

"*What I love about this book is that it challenges L&D professionals to approach their training programs with intention and curiosity. Rather than continuously using the same 'elements' in their work, trainers can use this book to find new ones that better suit the content, the learners, or the context. Jam-packed with helpful tools,* What's Your Formula? *will remind trainers that each program they create is its own unique experiment.*"

> —**Sophie Oberstein**, Author, *Troubleshooting for Trainers*

"What's Your Formula? *is a narrative in organizing and building an effective training program that guides you to answer a key question: What is the problem to solve? Like a baker, Washburn identifies different training elements and shows how to mix them together to create meaningful learning experiences.*"

> —**Tim Cunningham**, Director, Customer Training and Development,
> at a multinational tire manufacturing company

D1452515

BRIAN WASHBURN

WHAT'S YOUR FORMULA?

COMBINE LEARNING ELEMENTS FOR IMPACTFUL TRAINING

PRESS

Alexandria, VA

ATD Press is an internationally renowned source of insightful and practical information on talent development, training, and professional development.

ATD Press
1640 King Street
Alexandria, VA 22314 USA

Ordering information: Books published by ATD Press can be purchased by visiting ATD's website at td.org/books or by calling 800.628.2783 or 703.683.8100.

Library of Congress Control Number: 2021935241

ISBN-10: 1-952157-47-1
ISBN-13: 978-1-952157-47-9
e-ISBN: 978-1-952157-48-6

ATD Press Editorial Staff
Director: Sarah Halgas
Manager: Melissa Jones
Content Manager, Eliza Blanchard: Learning & Development
Developmental Editor: Kathryn Stafford
Text Design: Shirley E.M. Raybuck and Kathleen Dyson
Cover Design: Amanda Hudson, Faceout Studio

Printed by BR Printers, San Jose, CA

To River,

this book wouldn't exist if you hadn't been
craving corndogs that day.

To Quinn,

this book wouldn't exist if you hadn't wanted
to go to DC for spring break.

And to everyone

who embraces this butterfly effect-like journey
that we call life, open to pondering the question:
what's possible?

Contents

Introduction

What's Possible?

It's a question that both scientists and learning professionals should be asking themselves, nonstop: What's possible?

Dedicated scientists combine their expertise, developed through years of study, hard work, research, experimentation, observation, trial and error, and sheer curiosity, to mix elements and accomplish feats like curing disease or putting people on the moon.

If you believe in your craft as a learning professional, you can string some elements together and do this too. Seriously. A well-designed training program can be world changing. It can lead audience members to new knowledge, skills, or abilities that enable them to cure blindness, end child abuse, or figure out ways to curb or stop climate change. I've seen it happen. I've been part of training programs that have helped restore sight to blind people, enabled abused and neglected children find safe and permanent homes, and helped farmers improve their practices through sustainable crop planning.

A well-designed learning program can change the way individuals and organizations do things. Even if you're not working on projects that cure disease or lead to world peace, chances are you're working on something that will impact people. People spend more waking hours at work than they do anywhere else during the week, so when you can help someone do something new or differently or better, it can lead to higher job satisfaction, more efficient ways of working, and perhaps less time at the office. If your learning program can accomplish any of this, then you're influencing your learners' quality of life—you're changing *their* world.

Just as scientists use elements—such as hydrogen (H), gold (Au), or oganesson (Og)—as they study, research, or make world-changing breakthroughs in the fuels that take us to outer space or the electronics we carry in our pockets, we as learning professionals rely on combining different elements in our field.

We may need to string together elements such as adult learning (Al), lesson plans (Lp), Mr. Sketch markers (Ms), and gamification (Gm) to develop engaging learning experiences that help people want to do something new or differently or better. When we find the right combination of elements and people walk away from something we've designed with new skills and abilities, we change lives.

Engaging, effective training programs are a mixture of science and art; they require a certain quantity of adult learning theory, available technology, intuitive tools, proven practices, and creativity, and a touch of risk. Finding the right combinations and proportions of these elements, however, depends on the situation.

With all of this in mind, an idea struck me when I was at a restaurant one day. My oldest child had ordered corndogs from the kids' menu, which came with a placemat printed with a periodic table of tasty ingredients. As I looked at the placemat, I began to wonder what an equivalent periodic table of engaging and effective learning elements might look like. Over the next days and weeks, an image began to emerge in my mind, and I began to ask my colleagues for their thoughts on instructional design and training elements that could fall under the metaphor of "solids" and "liquids" and "gas-like" elements. That corndog-filled lunch, some individual brainstorming time, and collaboration with my co-workers led to the creation of the Periodic Table of Amazing Learning Experiences (Figure I-1). While it has undergone several iterations, the fun part about this visual metaphor is that users can combine various elements strategically and intentionally to yield amazing learning experiences.

I've been in the learning and development field long enough to have heard all sorts of predictions. The ease and consistency of e-learning will eliminate the need for instructor-led training. Virtual meeting platforms will eliminate the need (and cost) of traveling to on-site, in-person training. The creation of the chief learning officer role will give the learning function "a seat at the table" and transform how organizations learn. The learning management system will ensure the availability of individualized learning, anywhere, anytime. MOOCs, free online courses from some of the world's leading universities, will forever disrupt the way both higher ed and corporate training conduct business. Bold predictions are a dime a dozen, and none of these quite panned out the way some "futurists" in our industry thought they might.

Figure I-1. Periodic Table of Amazing Learning Experiences

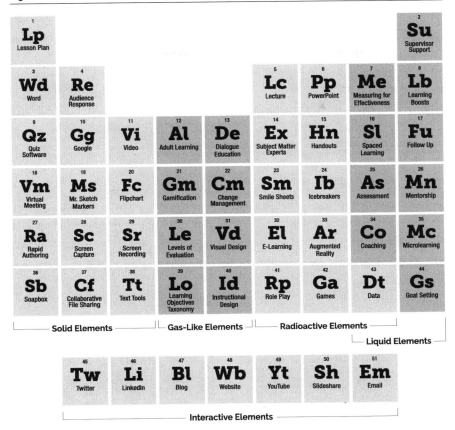

Of course, e-learning, virtual meeting platforms, LMSs, and MOOCs were all important innovations in our field. How do we track and make sense of them? And what about our old, trusted tools and models? Is there still a place for them?

The periodic table of learning elements that you'll find in this book is an attempt to say: Yes, new innovations and time-tested strategies and practices all play a role. To help sort through the plethora of options available to trainers and learning experience designers, I organized this periodic table into solids, liquids, gases, radioactive elements, and interactive elements. Some elements have been around for a long time; others have only recently been discovered. You may look at the table and think of other elements that are not represented, or you may find that it inspires you to dream up some yet-to-be-discovered elements. The point of this table is to offer up tools and strategies that, when combined under certain conditions, have the potential to create amazing learning experiences for your participants. They are that impactful. You just need to know how to harness their dynamic properties, and that's what this book can help you do. Whether you're new to the field of learning and development or you've been doing this for years, I hope the way in which this table is organized can inspire new ideas and ways to organize the design of your learning programs.

How you choose to string together some of these elements of amazing learning experiences—the way in which you "find your formula" for a specific learning program—is often much more art than science. Yes, you should incorporate evidence-based practices as much as possible, but when you're working with humans, making sure you mix the science of learning with the art of learning experience design will be very important. And that's how this book can be most helpful.

As you grow more familiar with the range of elements across this periodic table, you may begin to experiment with a variety of combinations, almost the same way that scientists create chemical equations. For example, a shorthand way to think through the combination of a set of gas-like elements, solid elements, and a radioactive element to yield an effective e-learning program could look something like this:

$$El = (Lo + Al) + (Vi + Ra) + Ex$$

While *What's Your Formula?* uses the science-inspired metaphor of a periodic table as the core theme, it is not intended to be a book about the science behind how people learn. You will find some references to data, statistics, and research throughout these pages, but there are a number of excellent publications written by a lot of very smart people that will take you through the science of learning in much more depth. If it's the science of learning you'd like to dive into more deeply, then one or more of the following may prove helpful to you:

- *Evidence-informed Learning Design: Creating Training to Improve Performance* (Mirjam Neelen and Paul A. Kirschner)
- *Transfer of Training: Action-Packed Strategies to Ensure High Payoff from Training Investments* (Mary L. Broad and John W. Newstrom)

- *E-Learning and the Science of Instruction: Proven Guidelines for Consumers and Designers of Multimedia Learning* (Ruth Colvin Clark and Richard E. Mayer)
- *Design for How People Learn* (Julie Dirksen)

About This Book

In chapter 1, we examine the gas-like elements. These are eight core concepts, models, and theories that you may never actually be able to see, but are typically wafting through the air of any training room. While most people don't really notice if these gas-like elements are present (kind of how we very rarely think too much about the oxygen that surrounds us every day), it will become very evident very quickly if we walk into a stuffy or suffocating learning environment where no gas-like elements have been provided. The gas-like elements become the building blocks for everything else you read in this book.

Chapter 2 explores 10 different liquid elements, which are practices primarily designed to support knowledge and skill transfer. They have been categorized as "liquid" because they can be quite flexible and often take the shape of the vessel (individuals, teams, organizations) into which they are poured. Of course, their flexibility also allows you to freeze them in place if you think they can be a solid pillar of a learning program (and if things change, you can melt them down again and change them up).

In chapter 3, we put 11 radioactive elements under the microscope to determine if your learning program can be powered for years by harnessing these tools, practices, and resources . . . or if your design or program is unintentionally emitting toxic learning experiences that can contaminate the reputation of your learning team for generations to come. Perhaps "generations to come" is tongue-in-cheek hyperbole, but do take great care when using these elements, because when they're misused, they really do diminish the prestige and credibility of your learning programs.

In chapter 4, we take a look at the solid elements of amazing learning experiences. You'll explore 15 different tools—some of which are physical (thus the term "solid elements") while others which are digital—that you may wish to use as you develop your next learning program.

Chapter 5 reviews seven different interactive elements. These internet-based social media and communication platforms enable learning to go well beyond the traditional training room or learning management system, encouraging learners to interact with one another as well as the rest of the world.

Beyond these periodic elements, effective training programs depend on an X factor: your comfort level as a designer or facilitator with engaging learners. In chapter 6 we take a closer look at the impact that a facilitator—whether you're designing for yourself or for someone else to deliver the content—can have on an overall learning program. As you'll find out, your training design should look very different based upon the facilitator's level of content knowledge and ability to apply adult learning principles to their presentation delivery.

Chapter 7, "Finding the Right Formula," puts together everything you've learned throughout this book. It features a series of real-life case examples; you'll be challenged to determine which elements were present in the right quantities, which elements were overused, and which elements may have been missing. You'll put yourself in the place of the person putting the programs in each scenario together, and decide which other elements to include. Once you reflect upon each situation, you'll be able to see how your thoughts compared to what actually happened. Perhaps some of these scenarios will resemble situations that you've had to confront in your own work. Even if you've never had to face any of these scenarios, chances are good that you'll find some transferable lessons in one or more of these situations.

Sometimes books, especially business books like this, feel a bit like a lecture. They're presented in an (I hope) interesting format and they're full of (I hope good) information. We read them, perhaps highlighting some key points or dog earing a few pages, and then we put them on a shelf.

I strove to bring learning design into the way this book was structured in hopes that you could relate what you've read to your own situation and learning programs. At the end of each chapter, you'll find an opportunity to reflect on how you're currently using any of the elements discussed and identify whether and how you may want to integrate other elements into your program.

Some of you may choose to read this book from start to finish to gain a better understanding of all these elements and how they fit together. Others may choose to scan the table of contents and flip to the elements you think would be most applicable to you in your moment of need. However you choose to use this book—as a cover-to-cover page-turner or as a workbook in which you capture all of your thoughts and reflections or as a quick reference guide—I hope you'll find new elements that will help you engage your learners in professional development experiences that ultimately lead to change. I also hope this book can help you to find new answers you may have never dreamed of when you've asked yourself the question: What's possible?

Experiment away, try new things, and don't get discouraged if they blow up in your face. That's what experimentation is all about. It's how new breakthroughs are discovered. Learn, adjust, and try again.

Whether you're just breaking into the field of learning and development or you've been working in the field for decades, I hope this book will help you find (or rediscover) a sense of adventure and fearlessness when it comes to meeting your learners' needs. I hope this book helps you find your formula.

Chapter 1
Gas-Like Elements

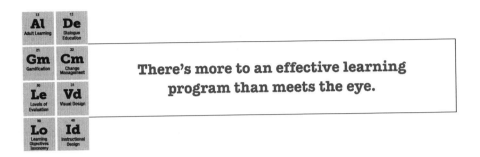

There's more to an effective learning program than meets the eye.

In my first instructional design role, I didn't even know I was an instructional designer. I was teaching at a youth center, helping youth in Washington, DC, who had dropped out of school get their high school equivalency credential (GED), and I would spend my afternoons putting together a lesson plan for the next day.

When I was promoted to lead the whole GED portion of our team, including supervising several other GED instructors, I realized I needed to find some help. So, I turned to my father, who had spent years not only as a classroom instructor but as the guy who led training programs at our school district to help other teachers be more effective. I remember sitting around the dinner table and getting a kick out of my father's job: teaching teachers how to teach.

Now it was my turn. I needed a crash course on teaching so I could make sure that all the other GED teachers also knew how to teach, so I called up my dad and asked for some pointers on curriculum design. Several days later, I got a package in the mail full of binders, books, and notes on how to use it all.

All I *thought* I wanted was to know how to put a few lesson plans together. What I *learned*, however, was that a comprehensive learning program is more than just lesson plans. It's more than just handouts and games like Jeopardy and creative ideas and bringing people to the whiteboard or the flipchart. It was more than just having the desire to keep people engaged.

An effective learning program required intentionality. I couldn't simply lecture on what I wanted to talk about based on something I'd read the prior evening. I shouldn't simply pop in a review game because I thought it might be fun. Well, I could actually do either of these things, but only if they fit into the bigger picture learning objectives I created.

I had a hunch that people better and smarter than me had done this stuff in the past, but I had never been exposed to any formal study of the practices, theories, or research on what truly made for effective learning experiences. I needed to better learn how people learn, how to identify needs, and how to develop learner-centered, action-oriented objectives if I wanted to do right by my students. I needed to figure out a variety of ways to determine if they were learning, and I had to determine how to make any changes that came about from that knowledge.

There was way more to an effective learning experience than I ever imagined, but I couldn't *see* what the best teachers I'd had growing up or the best trainers I'd learned from during conferences were doing as they put their programs together. Perhaps one of the most important lessons I've ever learned while putting together educational experiences was that I needed to make real what I couldn't see.

Enter the gas-like elements.

What Are Gas-Like Elements?

We begin our in-depth exploration of the Periodic Table of Amazing Learning Experiences by putting the big-picture, all-encompassing gas-like elements under the microscope. Gas-like elements are concepts, models, and theories that you may never see, but that constantly waft through the air of any training room. Some, like the air we breathe, are invisible and odorless, but you'd definitely know if they were suddenly vacuumed out of the training room. Without one or more of these elements constantly swirling around your learning programs, none of the other elements matter. There are eight gas-like elements: adult learning (Al), dialogue education (De), gamification (Gm), change management (Cm), levels of evaluation (Le), visual design (Vd), learning objectives taxonomy (Lo), and instructional design (Id).

In any quality adult learning (Al) experience, you must include the work of titans such as Malcolm Knowles and Robert Gagné. Perhaps less well-known—because their contributions to the field are newer—but no less important is the work of Jane Vella (dialogue education, De); Cammie Bean and Cathy Moore (instructional design, Id); Donald Kirkpatrick and Will

Thalheimer (levels of evaluation, Le); Nancy Duarte and Melissa Marshall (visual design, Vd); and Karl Kapp, Kevin Werbach, and Dan Hunter (gamification, Gm).

Without integrating their work into your training program, a game will be just a time-consuming activity, not part of a truly gamified experience; the usefulness of smile sheet data will be limited because you're not asking the right questions; and slides will continue to be repositories for presenters' knowledge, not visual experiences that help learners more easily digest and process information.

 ## Element 12
Adult Learning (Al)

Adult learning theory, also known as *andragogy*, has been around for a long, long time but is perhaps best characterized by the work of Malcolm Knowles. *The Adult Learner*, which was published in 1973 (and has been updated several times since), is his most well-known book.

Depending on which source you cite, there are three, four, six, or seven key principles that characterize the adult learner. For the purposes of this discussion, the key properties of element 12, adult learning, are:

- Adults come into the training room with previous life and work experience.
- Adult learners are autonomous and self-directed learners.
- Adult learners need to see and understand the relevance of what's being taught.
- Adult learners want to be able to use what's being taught to solve a problem in the near future.

So, what does this mean in plain English? Basically, if we want a learning experience to truly be amazing, we can't just get up in front of a group and start sharing content. We need to be intentional about what needs to be learned and how we present that information, all depending on who our audience is. For every learning experience, we need to reflect upon and answer some basic questions such as:

- How am I honoring the previous life and work experiences of my participants?
- What choices will I allow my participants to make during this learning experience?

- How will the relevance of my topic to my participants be made crystal clear?
- Will my participants know how to use my information to solve a problem by the end of the experience?

Perhaps more so than any other element in this gas-like category, when principles of adult learning are missing from a learning experience, it truly is as if the oxygen has been sucked out of the room. After a while, the absence of adult learning principles makes it uncomfortable, almost impossible to take in a dull, meandering presentation.

On the bright side, it's been my experience that a lot of people know of the term *adult learning*. I've worked with a number of department heads and subject matter experts who have all said that they embrace adult learning and would like to see it woven throughout their learning programs.

The idea that adults should be at the center of their own learning experience, that they should be given autonomy (to some degree) over what happens in a training program, that they need relevant content, and that the content needs to solve a work-related problem is not controversial. However, it's also been my experience that while department heads and subject matter experts say they embrace adult learning, very few are equipped with the knowledge and the skills to actually put these principles into action.

This is where talent development professionals need to shine. Subject matter experts and department heads aren't paid to know how to put principles of adult learning into action, and we shouldn't be frustrated by this fact. We need to take advantage of the fact that there are department heads and subject matter experts who are open to incorporating principles of adult learning into their training programs, and then we need to help them design learning programs that honor these principles.

You can show what's possible when adult learning is integrated into each learning experience in many ways. Bonding principles of adult learning with the following elements can offer some ideas on where and how to begin:

- **Lecture (Lc).** When you design through the lens of adult learning, even the traditional lecture can look different. Asking a rhetorical question at the beginning of a lecture can give the audience an immediate clue to how the content can help them solve a problem. Incorporating a tightly woven story can make content seem more real and help listeners see the relevance. Keep in mind that lecture doesn't always have to be synonymous with a machine-like reading of facts and figures from the podium. In fact, if you're honoring the principles of adult learning, it never should by synonymous with that.

- **PowerPoint (Pp).** A quick way to integrate principles of adult learning into PowerPoint slides is to ensure that the relevance of each slide is clear. Sometimes this can be done by limiting the amount of text on a slide, highlighting key words when text cannot be limited, and ensuring imagery correlates to what's being discussed. More advanced users of PowerPoint may choose to include hyperlinks on their slides and allow participants to choose the order in which certain topics are covered, giving them autonomy and allowing them to identify the most relevant topics.

- **Learning boosts (Lb).** It's one thing to help learners understand the relevance of a topic when they're immersed in a learning experience, whether it's in-person or an e-learning course. Sending learning boosts after the initial learning experience has concluded is another opportunity to keep content relevant, build upon initial concepts, and help learners identify how the content can solve work-related problems.

- **Google (Gg).** There may be (many) times when formal training programs are not necessary. Reminding and encouraging learners to take control over their learning and professional development by conducting their own research using Google or other available resources allows them to find what they need in the flow of their workday.

- **Subject matter experts (Ex).** Keep in mind that nobody on the planet actually carries a business card listing "subject matter expert" as their job title. Subject matter experts have day jobs and are usually paid to make money for the organization by doing something other than training. So, if you're able to help craft a message or lesson plan for your subject matter experts that abides by the principles of adult learning, you can support them and help ensure learners are exposed to meaningful learning experiences.

- **Change management (Cm).** If you're working with an organization that understands the need to integrate adult learning theory into learning programs, then your life may be much easier. If you're working with organizations that either have not bought in to, have not heard of, or claim they don't have time for "touchy feely" concepts like adult learning theory, then change will be necessary, and it's not likely to happen quickly. Change management components such as identifying the need to integrate adult learning into a program and identifying key influencers such as a department head or subject matter expert who would be open to the change are important initial steps. Designing programs that integrate key principles of adult learning to show the rest of the organization what's possible may be necessary, because just talking about theory and dropping Malcolm Knowles' name into your conversation won't move the needle on this.

- **E-learning (El).** E-learning offers an almost-endless opportunity for learners to autonomously choose certain paths during a learning experience and simulate real-world applications of key concepts. The key to effective e-learning that provides an amazing learning experience, even when under tight deadlines and without a large budget, is to ask: How can I ensure the relevance of this content cannot be missed or mistaken?

- **Virtual meeting (Vm).** Virtual meeting platforms offer a variety of tools to help you connect the relevance of your content to the actual learning experience. While smaller group sizes allow for more breakout rooms or discussion using voice or chat features, even webinars attended by hundreds or thousands of people can integrate polling, storytelling, rhetorical questions, or discussion prompts with which learners can engage and decide for themselves how they can use your content.

- **Collaborative file sharing (Cf).** Emphasizing the fundamental idea that adult learners are autonomous, being able to quickly find internal documents, policies, forms, and resources without having to go through an entire formal training program is a strategy that respects an employee's ability to think for themselves. Confirming the collaborative file sharing repository is up-to-date and easily searchable will help ensure this element can be effectively used.

- **Learning objectives taxonomy (Lo).** Honoring the key principles of adult learning begins with learning objectives. Are they learner-centric? Are you using verbs that will lead to learning activities that truly accomplish what your training program is supposed to do?

Element 13
Dialogue Education (De)

Influenced heavily by the concept of adult learning theory, dialogue education is an element that was brought to the public's attention by educator Jane Vella, who believed that dialogue is the cornerstone of how learning happens. In her book *Learning to Listen, Learning to Teach: The Power of Dialogue in Educating Adults*, Vella outlines the 12 core properties of this element:

1. **Needs assessment.** Who needs what according to whom?

2. **Safety.** How can we make sure all learners experience an environment in which their contribution is valued?

3. **Sound relationships.** Everyone in the learning experience is in some sort of relationship with one another, and there should be genuine curiosity that runs both ways in each of these relationships—instructor to learner, learner to learners, designer to learners.

4. **Sequence and reinforcement.** The flow of a learning experience matters and needs to be intentional, and key concepts shouldn't be touched upon only once with the assumption they've left a meaningful impact on the learners.

5. **Praxis.** From the Greek word for *practice with reflection*, this concept reflects that it's not just enough to have learners go through an activity—the debriefing of that activity is at least as important as the activity itself.

6. **Learners as decision makers.** Do we respect our learners enough to allow them to make some decisions about their learning experience?

7. **Ideas, feelings, and actions.** It's not enough to be exposed to a concept; learners need to have an emotional connection and decide when, if, and how to act upon the concepts and emotions.

8. **Immediacy.** Will the content help learners do their job better (tomorrow)? Will it help solve a problem (today)?

9. **Clear roles.** Another name for this principle could be humility; does the presenter feel the need to be "the professor" in front of the room, holding a monopoly on all knowledge, or do learners play a role in the dialogue that takes place in the learning experience?

10. **Teamwork.** In accordance with the idea that two (or three or four) heads are better than one, providing opportunities for learners

to work together not only aids in in-the-moment learning, but also mirrors real life, in which people generally need to work with colleagues across an organization to get things done.

11. **Engagement of the learners.** When learners are deeply engaged in a learning experience, especially one that revolves around dialogue, it can be difficult to get them to *stop* learning.

12. **Accountability.** Yes, learners need to ultimately be accountable for their learning and what they do after a learning experience, but facilitators and course designers must also be accountable to the learners, putting the effort in to ensure an engaging, purposeful experience.

While a firm grasp of these concepts is important, you don't need to memorize all 12. When I introduce dialogue education during a train-the-trainer session, I'll often ask participants, if they had to choose one of these concepts, which do they think is the *most* important? After they share their thoughts, the room always fills with relieved laughter when I tell them that no single concept is most important. But by being asked to read through descriptions of each and make a value judgment about which is best, they better understand them. Through the ensuing dialogue of this activity, we all learn, which is the whole point of dialogue education.

Think of some of the learning programs or presentations you've designed or given. Which of these 12 concepts did you apply, perhaps even without thinking about it? Which came most naturally?

Now think of the same learning programs or presentations. Which of these concepts might have been missing? How would the program or presentation be different, possibly even better, if some concepts were more overtly present?

In an effort to help with this last set of questions, dialogue education can be bonded with some of the following elements to better ensure that you're able to bring all 12 concepts into your next learning program:

- **Audience response (Re).** Whether you're in front of a large group or a handful of people, finding ways for learners to engage with your content and with one another can be key. Audience response tools allow your learners to vote, share their thoughts, or respond to your questions in a way that is safe (it's generally anonymous) and allows everyone's voice to be seen and heard.

- **Lesson plan (Lp).** We cover this concept in depth in chapter 2, but when you are able to map out the sequence and flow of your activities—complete with talking points, instructional techniques, and detailed directions—the odds of intentionally incorporating the concepts of dialogue education increase over simply putting together your presentation by opening up PowerPoint and generating a slide deck.
- **Assessment (As).** Common tools of assessment include formal quizzing or testing, but through dialogue, you can quickly and informally gauge how well your learners are "getting it."
- **E-learning (El).** While Jane Vella's original concepts focused on in-person instruction, the fundamentals of dialogue education can be brought into e-learning design with great success. Integrating comments, vignettes, scenario-based interactions, and case studies that include real dialogue from others are ways to asynchronously expose people to others' experiences. Integrating discussion boards could be an alternate way to asynchronously bring dialogue into a learning experience between people who may be half a world away.
- **Virtual meeting (Vm).** While dialogue with participants can be increasingly difficult as the attendance of a virtual meeting grows, most platforms offer a variety of ways to include the voice of participants and allow them to enter into dialogue with the facilitator as well as between one another. Using breakout rooms, the chat tool, on-screen annotation, or allowing participants to come off mute to speak with the facilitator or other participants are all ways to design dialogue into a virtual meeting.

Element 21
Gamification (Gm)

There is a difference between element 42 (games) and element 21 (gamification). Games—as you'll read in chapter 3, "Radioactive Elements"—are something you play, and are often isolated activities within a larger learning experience. Gamification, on the other hand, is an intentional design strategy applied to some or all of a learning experience.

If you're curious whether your learning program has truly "gamified" the experience for your learners, you may want to ask whether it has any combination of these gamification properties:

- Engages learners by carrying game-based elements throughout the design of a learning experience
- Balances content delivery and game play in an ongoing basis
- Introduces or reinforces new knowledge, skills, or abilities

But, what are these "game-based elements"? Points are perhaps the most commonly used—get an answer correct, you get points; get it incorrect, you lose points. Once you've reached a certain number of points, or perhaps if you have the most points at the end of the game, you (and your team) win.

Another commonly used game-based element is the leaderboard. You keep accruing points over time and see how you stack up against colleagues, peers, co-workers, people in other offices, and so forth. Points can be carried over a multiday in-person session or can be tracked in a learning management system that shows a leaderboard over time.

Badges are yet another commonly used game element. Accrue enough points, complete enough courses, or hit a certain score on an end-of-course test and you've earned a badge. Can you collect every badge offered across our training offerings?

These three game elements can offer incentive and create new streams of engagement for learners, especially those who thrive on competition and achievements, and those who like to play games outside work. However, relying solely on points, leaderboards, and badges in an overall gamification strategy is a bit like relying on hamburgers, tacos, and pizza for a nutritional strategy. They're easy, but relying exclusively on them means you're missing out on a lot of other effective game elements; eventually you and your learners may get tired of what you're serving up.

In their book *For the Win: How Game Design Can Revolutionize Your Business*, Kevin Werbach and Dan Hunter outline a whole host of other game elements to include in any gamification design and strategy:

- **Constraints.** Can you accomplish the goal of an activity or game within the rules and limited resources available?
- **Emotions.** Can you get so wrapped up in an activity that it makes you feel how certain concepts can influence the outcome?
- **Narrative or storyline.** When we chose to gamify the new employee onboarding process at one organization where I worked, we used the organization's mission statement as the overall narrative (how can we eliminate corneal blindness throughout the world?).

Then we incorporated a short game that represented the work of each department to illustrate how everyone worked toward the organization's overall mission.

- **Relationships.** Can there be meaningful interactions among all learners and game players that demonstrate how we're all in this together?
- **Elements of chance.** Think *Jeopardy* and the "Daily Double." It's hiding somewhere on the board, and the only way you'll find it (and perhaps double your score) is if you keep answering questions correctly and control the board.
- **Competition or cooperation.** While in chapter 5 I talk more about competitive and cooperative games, keep in mind that gamification doesn't have to mean that people or teams are competing against each other. Sometimes your learning objectives are better served when everyone works together to "beat the game."
- **Feedback.** How do you know that you made a correct or incorrect choice? In some games you win (or lose) points. In some scenario-based games, your avatar gets stronger (or, with poor choices, can die). In a finance-related game, perhaps your bank account increases with each correct answer, or you go bankrupt. In an ethics-related game, you could lose your job or the organization may lose all credibility. Feedback doesn't have to simply be text that says "right" or "wrong"; the power of gamification-based feedback is that it can *show* and allow learners to *experience* consequences.
- **Resource acquisition.** Sometimes a learning experience is enhanced when players can accrue different resources beyond just points. Perhaps in a gamified learning experience focused on sales, you can accrue new contacts, additional "credibility points," and a larger expense account as you navigate trickier and more complex sales scenarios.
- **Transactions between players.** Sometimes learning how to work together means that players can trade resources they've accrued with others involved in the learning experience so they can benefit one another. Bringing a gamified experience to this level not only helps learners grasp new concepts but teaches them concepts and interpersonal skills that can't always be effectively taught by other methods.
- **Boss fights and culminating challenges.** If you've ever played a video game (*Super Mario Bros.* for example), you know that bouncing

on top of killer tortoiseshells and jumping over bottomless pits are just the warm-up challenges; to clear the level, you need to get past a bigger, tougher final opponent. Similarly, in a learning experience, it may help to warm up learners with smaller challenges before they need to combine everything they've learned to complete a culminating activity.

- **Levels.** Just like real life, when you've moved past one culminating activity, the door is simply unlocked to bigger and even more complex concepts and skills.

There are lots more, and if you'd like to read in more depth about gamification, I also recommend Karl Kapp's *The Gamification of Learning and Instruction: Game-Based Methods and Strategies for Training and Education.*

The bottom line is that simply dropping an activity that uses points to determine how well participants did may give your learners a whiff of a "game," but unless it's part of a more comprehensive design strategy woven throughout the learning experience, you haven't quite infused the program with the pleasant, wafting aroma of a fully baked gamified experience. The following elements can be bonded with gamification to help design a more complete and comprehensive gamified learning experience:

- **Quiz software (Qz).** Using quiz software such as Kahoot during a training session can be a fun way to introduce topics or engage learners in review activity. The system does all the work when it comes to keeping track of points and leaders, all you need to do is fill in the questions and the content. To bring this beyond a game into the realm of gamification, you can use quiz software as one element in a series of challenges whereby your learners must achieve a minimum threshold score to continue their quest for knowledge and new skills, only unlocking the next piece of content once the threshold has been reached.
- **Video (Vi).** There are several ways video can play a part in a larger gamification initiative. First, presenting your learners with a challenge to generate learner-created content and share during a session or post as part of an online program can be a way to earn points or complete a challenge that unlocks additional content or feedback. Video can also be used to allow SMEs (or even actors) to present content as a clue or part of a game component that learners

need to piece together to uncover important content or be exposed to new skills.

- **Lesson plan (Lp).** As mentioned at the start of this section, a game is something you play, while gamification is an intentional design strategy. Using a lesson plan (or for e-learning, a storyboard) to map out that design strategy can help you connect the dots and envision how a completely gamified program could work.

- **Assessment (As).** Not only can you learn a lot about the answers and choices a participant makes during a gamified experience, but you can assess a lot about the learner and their ability to work with others and problem solve as well.

- **E-learning (El).** Using a comprehensive narrative to help a learner navigate an overall learning experience can bring relevance to individual games and activities throughout an e-learning experience.

- **Augmented reality (Ar).** When you think about the gamification of learning programs, there are a variety of technologies that can be helpful; encouraging participants to use their devices can broaden their learning opportunities. Integrating the element of augmented reality allows your participants to see things that aren't actually physically present in the training environment, which can add a unique touch to your training program. Take advantage of software tools like Zappar and send your participants on an augmented reality–based quest or scavenger hunt as part of a broader gamification initiative.

- **Learning objectives taxonomy (Lo).** The key to success for a gamified learning initiative—and the element that will ensure a fun, engaging experience is also a valuable, effective experience—is the learning objectives taxonomy that's used, and specifically the learning objectives that have been defined for the program. If the activities don't align with the best way to accomplish the learning objectives, then gamified or not, it's not an effective learning program.

- **Games (Ga).** It would be very difficult to generate a gamified learning experience without the use of games. However, you need to remember that games—even if you put a series of games into one learning experience—are not synonymous with gamification. The games chosen, the game-like elements integrated, and the comprehensive nature of a learning experience are the pieces that need to be combined to create a truly gamified experience.

Element 22
Change Management (Cm)

Learning initiatives without change management strategies are a bit like the world without hydrogen or helium; there's just no lift.

When I became a training professional, I was very excited to get in front of a group and present, using a flipchart I had made or activities I'd come up with to meet the learning objectives. People would see me at conferences or other events, and they'd come up and tell me that they still remembered a training program I had delivered a year or two earlier. It was exciting, and my ego grew . . . until I began to ask a simple question: "That's great to hear! What kinds of things did you change after the training session?"

They'd pause for a moment and think, then their response would go something like this: "You know, I can't tell you specifics, but I really liked your training. It was one of the best I've ever been part of!"

That was the response I dreaded most. It frustrated me because training isn't just about engaging people and making sure they enjoy the learning experience. At the end of the day, if an organization is investing time and money for someone to go through a training experience, it should result in some sort of behavior change or new skill adopted. This is where change management comes in.

Change management is a process in which intention is applied and an environment is created to help a person or organization do something new, different, or better. A number of models have been developed to guide a person or organization through sustainable change, but at its core, change management is characterized by:

- A structured process
- A design with the intention to make adjustments sustainable

Notice the word "sustainable"; it's not meant to be permanent. While effective change management is intended to move a person or organization from a current to a future state, progress can always be made and additional changes may need to be facilitated in the future.

Change management is an underlying piece of ATD's Talent Development Capability Model, an element that is significant in the Impacting Organizational Capability. While this is often thought of more as a specialty of organization development practitioners, anyone involved in training and instructional design should at least have a foundational understanding of the key concepts and models beneath change management. This is because:

- **Individual change leads to greater confidence.** When participants learn a new skill or take away a job aid that helps them immediately solve a problem, they will generally be more willing to try other new things. With appropriate individual change management strategies in place, learning experiences can become a virtuous cycle.

- **Seeing is believing.** When needed change is observed happening in the halls of an organization, it builds champions among department heads, executives, and key influencers. These are the people who approve future learning initiatives, and they're good allies to have, but we in turn must show them that our learning initiatives can be effective.

- **Sustainable change means demonstrable value.** Whether a training initiative to implement a new sales model leads to increased sales or a learning program built to break down perceived silos leads to increased communication and higher employee satisfaction scores, measurable changes in individual and organizational behaviors can lead to important case studies and justification for the value of future learning initiatives.

Here are two of the most commonly used models of change management:

- **John Kotter's 8-Step Change Model** follows eight sequential steps that allow sustainable change to occur (there are no shortcuts for sustainable change):
  - Create a sense of urgency.
  - Form a powerful guiding coalition.
  - Create a vision for the change.
  - Enlist a volunteer army aligned with the change.
  - Remove barriers to enable action.
  - Generate and communicate short-term wins.
  - Accelerate the change.
  - Institutionalize the change.

- **Prosci's ADKAR Framework** helps individuals move through organizational change by navigating five steps:
  - Awareness of the need for change
  - Desire to support the change

- Knowledge of how to change
- Ability to demonstrate skills and behaviors
- Reinforcement to make the change stick

Regardless of the model you choose or the structure you apply to ensure an environment in which sustainable change is possible, keep in mind that individual and organization change do not happen in a neat, straight line such as this:

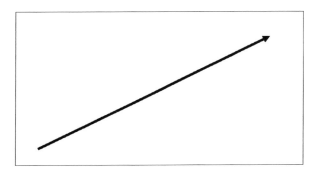

Actual individual and organization change will typically look more like:

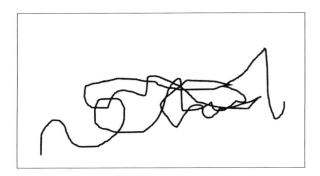

And that's when you've put some effort into change management. This is why it's important to have a plan, be prepared for backsliding, and be persistent in your efforts. Also, you should keep in mind that learning initiatives generally aren't the only thing needed for organizational change—they often need to be coupled with other elements, even when trying to encourage individual change.

Entire master's degree-level programs are built around change management. It's important to find time to investigate the models and strategies, but when it comes to other elements that can be bonded with change management to amplify its effect, consider the impact of:

- **Supervisor support (Su).** This is covered in much more detail in chapter 2, but there is a significant body of research that points to the fact that if you want someone to apply what they've learned in a training program, their supervisor will be the most important factor. Identifying ways to engage the supervisor, whether you're providing goal-setting resources or just communicating what's possible from the training program, is essential if you want the program to have a chance to bring sustainable change.

- **Measuring for effectiveness (Me).** Finding ways to assess the program's effectiveness is the most tangible way to measure for impact and behavior change. This begins with identifying baseline data against which post-training data can be compared.

- **Follow up (Fu).** While supervisor support is crucial, so is direct follow up with learners. Every change model includes a step related to maintaining the momentum that can be established through small victories. Your learners may be extremely motivated to apply new knowledge or skills when they're in the moment of learning, but follow up, once they return to their regular workflow, will be an important contributor to long-term behavior change.

- **Levels of evaluation (Le).** Having a variety of data points can help identify the efficacy of a change initiative at any given point in time. Knowing how many people participated in a session, what their reaction to the program was, how much they may have learned, whether they've been able to apply anything to their job, what the impact has been, and whether there has been any measurable return on the investment are all pieces of information that can be examined for a more complete picture of whether and to what degree a change has taken place.

- **Learning objectives taxonomy (Lo).** If you want to change specific behaviors, that should be documented from the beginning of the design process. The learning objectives that are chosen and the activities connected to them will be all you have to steer your learners in the right direction.

- **Instructional design (Id).** If change is the ultimate goal, then the need for that change should be assessed from the beginning and strategies to support it—such as baseline data, program evaluation, goal setting, making the case for change during the instruction, supervisor support, and follow up—need to be part of the overall program design.

- **Data (Dt).** Whether qualitative or quantitative, measurement determines the need for change and whether it has taken place.
- **Goal setting (Gs).** It's one thing to want to change; it's a whole other thing to have a specific idea of what needs to change. Offering learners an opportunity to reflect on where they may have knowledge or skills gaps, and what and how they can apply following the training program, is important. Preparing something for them to discuss with their supervisor as part of their goals is even more important.

Element 30
Levels of Evaluation (Le)

Have you ever collected end-of-training evaluation forms and, as soon as the last participant is out the door, hurried to scan through the comments? Lots of "that was the best training I've ever received" can absolutely make your day. Of course, reading "that was a total waste of time"—even if it's the only negative comment in 50 evaluation forms—can be soul crushing.

The thing is, those post-training evaluation forms are only one way to evaluate the program, and we shouldn't put too much weight on any particular evaluation component. Each one provides a data point that tells a story—the more data points, the more complete story we can tell.

Element 30, levels of evaluation, is characterized by three properties:

- Determines the effectiveness or success of a training program
- Uses qualitative and quantitative measures
- Gathered at various points between the actual training event and a specified time following the event

There are six commonly used levels of evaluation. Levels 1–4 are commonly attributed to Donald Kirkpatrick and collectively referred to as Kirkpatrick's Four Levels of Evaluation. Various attributions have been given to Levels 0 and 5, which may offer a more complete view, depending on how you use the data.

- **Level 0: Attendance or course completion.** Also referred to as the "butts-in-seats" metric, this level measures how many people attended a training course or completed an e-learning program. While high numbers may be little more than a vanity metric (the fact that you've trained 4,500 people in a year may mean you've been busy, but does it tell us how effective you were?), low numbers could lead decision makers to question the investment in developing certain training programs.

- **Level 1: Learner reaction.** Also commonly referred to as "smile sheets" (which you'll learn more about in chapter 3), this level of evaluation provides the first quantitative and qualitative glimpse at how a learning program has been received by the participants. High scores or effusive praise may indicate the course (or the instructor) was popular, but they don't guarantee that learning has happened or that new skills have been developed. Low scores, however, could mean that participants were turned off for some reason and may merit further investigation to decide whether changes to the program should be made.

- **Level 2: Knowledge gain or learning.** Measuring learning or knowledge gain is traditionally done using pre- and post-tests to compare what someone knew before the training program began with how they performed on a similar set of questions after the program ends. While this is a logical way to collect information, there is a danger of putting too much stock in post-test results, especially if the post-test is administered at the end of the training program while the information is still fresh. Giving a post-test several days or even a week after the program ends may provide a more accurate indicator of knowledge gain, although getting people to take a post-test after they've left the training room may be tricky.

The first three levels of evaluation are typically collected during a training event. The next three are generally monitored and measured at some point following a training event.

- **Level 3: Transfer to the job or behavior change.** Has the learner applied new knowledge or skills to their daily routine? This is typically measured in one of three ways.
  - First, you can send a post-training survey to the participants, asking them to report on anything they've applied from the training program. While this is an important data point to determine the effectiveness of a training initiative, there is danger in self-reporting because participants will typically want to make themselves look as good as possible.

- ◦ A second way to measure Level 3 is to send the participants' supervisors a survey asking if they've observed a change in behavior. This may be a more objective instrument, but the response rates from supervisors are typically lower.
- ◦ A third method is for someone to observe the participants in action and complete an observation form. This is often used in the education and early childhood sectors, where principals or instructional coaches will observe teachers in action and note observations, sometimes providing feedback as well.

- **Level 4: Results or impact.** Did the learning program yield the results you were hoping for? This can (kind of) be determined if baseline data has been collected and compared with post-training performance. For example, if a training program was designed to increase the adoption of a new computer system, did the adoption actually increase? If the program was intended to decrease the amount of rework in a manufacturing facility, did that happen following the training program? As with every other level of evaluation, you'll have to use some caution in looking at these results. Are you sure that training was the sole cause for any movement in the metrics? Correlations can be inferred, but causation is much harder to demonstrate.

- **Level 5: Return on investment.** This is perhaps the trickiest level to calculate, but some organizations insist on using ROI as a measure of training effectiveness and value. At Level 5, you're basically asking: How much did it cost to put together the training program, and by how much did it increase revenue or reduce costs? You may have a challenge determining the direct costs associated with putting together a training program, such as how much to allocate to training staff time, SME time, materials, and participants' time attending the program? On the other side of the equation, how much of a rise in revenue or reduction in cost is owed to the training program compared with a shift in market conditions, efficiencies gained in other organizational initiatives, or other factors?

As you can see, each level provides a glimpse of program effectiveness from a different point in time, and each level offers imperfect data. Keep in mind that not every training program needs to be measured at every level. To determine which levels are most appropriate for your next training initiative, you'll have to determine what you want success to look like. And be sure to ask that question before you begin designing the program. It's very difficult to collect baseline data, for example, after you've already launched the learning program.

As you think through how these levels of evaluation can integrate with the design of your learning program, you may want to bond this element with one or more of the following:

- **Supervisor support (Su).** When you find ways to enlist the support of your learners' supervisors, they can help the learners find the relevance and importance of your content, which can boost Level 1 scores. Supervisor observations are also key to a more objective Level 3 evaluation.
- **Audience response (Re).** While pre- and post-testing are perhaps the most common way to formally conduct Level 2 evaluations, there are many opportunities to gather in-the-moment data around how much and whether learning is taking place. Using audience response software can be an informal way to collect Level 1 (reaction) and Level 2 (knowledge) evaluation data.
- **Quiz software (Qz).** Similar to audience response tools, quiz software can help you gather Level 2 information during the flow of a training program. Most quiz software allows you to review participant results and generate reports after participants have completed the quiz (which is often conducted in the form of a game).
- **Dialogue education (De).** Similar to several other examples discussed, the element of dialogue education can be an intentional yet informal way to measure Levels 1 and 2 during the course of a training program. When participants are engaged in conversation and dialogue, it's much easier to observe how much they're picking up and retaining.
- **Learning objectives taxonomy (Lo).** Identifying the appropriate objectives on which to focus and connecting them with the appropriate activities is the only way to ensure you're able to accurately measure the right things.
- **Instructional design (Id).** As with everything else in this chapter, once you've determined which levels of evaluation are important, they should be part of the overall design of the learning program. Pre- and

post-tests will take up precious session time. Efforts at Level 3 and Level 4 evaluation should be announced and even designed as part of the overall program, meaning learners must respond to post-training surveys so you can collect that data before they receive their certificate of completion for the course.

- **Data (Dt).** While all levels of evaluation are data points, it may be necessary to collect other information before you can make sense of the evaluation results. Baseline data and data on outside factors can all offer greater context, which will make any data collected as part of the levels of evaluation more meaningful.

Element 31
Visual Design (Vd)

Which slide is easier for you to process, slide 1 or slide 2?

Slide 1   Slide 2

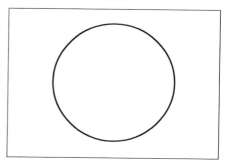

A simple closed shape in Euclidean geometry. It is the set of all points in a plane that are at a given distance from a given point, the center; equivalently it is the curve traced out by a point that moves so that its distance from a given point is constant.

This exercise was taken from a presentation, delivered by my friend Mike Taylor, entitled "A Few Things L&D Should Steal From the Marketing Department," and if you're anything like participants from his sessions, you'll agree that slide 2 is easier to process. It's simpler and more inviting.

The element of visual design may be overlooked and sometimes discarded because many of us are not natural graphic designers, and we're busy and just need some slides to accompany our amazingly designed content. If you're like me and have limited visual design instincts, you may want to try out a tool designed to help generate better slides and graphics. Some of the more popular visual design tools in use today include Canva, Visme, and Slidebean.

Let's take a closer look at this element, what it is, and why it may be more important that you'd think.

First, when we talk about visual design, we're talking about the environment we create when we put visual assets—PowerPoint slides, handouts, flip-charts, and job aids—on display for our learners. This element is characterized by one simple property: the intentional layout of visual imagery.

Good visual design often goes unnoticed, as if we collectively say: "We expected that." Poor visual design can be ignored by some, but rarely goes unnoticed. Let's look at four reasons why you ought to pay close attention to this element:

- **It establishes the tone.** Just by looking at your materials, will participants think that your session will be light and engaging? Verbose and dull? Visual design is often the first impression your learners will have of your program.
- **It sends a message.** Even when you think you're being unintentional, you're making a choice. It's a choice to spend time finding just the right image. It's a choice to adjust the font or color scheme or layout to be just right. It's a choice to scratch out some messaging on a flipchart at the last minute. It's a choice to take your time and prepare your visual imagery . . . or not.
- **It has the power to help everyone see themselves.** Do the people in your materials look like everyone who will go through your learning experience? It's very easy to just grab the first photo that seems to meet your needs, but "the first photo" typically shows a white businessperson. This is one of the most important (and often most overlooked) aspects of visual design. Can everyone see themselves in your materials?
- **It can make it easier to learn.** The first two images in this section about visual design presented the same information. One used a whole lot of text to describe a circle. The other used a simple image. There may be times when a detailed, technical narrative is the most appropriate way to share information. Then again, there are a lot more times when a simple visual image accompanied by verbal explanation, discussion, and dialogue can make it easier and more effective to learn. The less energy learners need to put into deciphering your visuals, the more energy they can put into actively engaging with you.

To prevent the common underuse of visual design, you may wish to bond this element with any of the following:

- **Word (Wd).** Microsoft Word is not a graphic design program, but that doesn't mean you can't put in the effort. Yes, some wonky things can happen with the formatting, especially when you try to combine documents, but well-designed, clearly laid out handouts, participant guides, and job aids are more inviting and more likely to be saved and used after a training session ends.

- **PowerPoint (Pp).** I'm always surprised by how many features are available in PowerPoint. In addition to the more popular features such as font, color, and layout choices, you can do some basic editing of images (removing items from the background, adjusting the color or transparency, and so forth) and basic cleanup of tables and charts to emphasize the data most important to your content and message.

- **Adult learning (Al).** Keep in mind that adult learning, at its core, is ensuring learners understand the relevance of your content to their lives. Economizing on words, emphasizing key concepts, and making sure any data presented is clearly labeled and reduces the amount of guesswork your learners need to engage in are all ways to bring adult learning theory into your visual design.

- **Flipchart (Fc).** When you choose to generate analog visual aids such as posters and flipcharts, be sure to take your time and prepare as much as you can in advance. Flipcharts can be powerful tools to which you and your learners refer all day.

- **Rapid authoring (Ra).** Rapid authoring tools have made it easy for anyone to generate e-learning modules. Keep in mind that simply because a tool is easy to use doesn't mean that you have a license to leave the learning materials ugly. Even when you're under time and budget pressures, taking some time to make sure the visual experience is clean and doesn't look like someone just used the default settings can make an impact on how your learners perceive the credibility of your course and your content.

Element 39
Learning Objectives Taxonomy (Lo)

The first thing you may be asking is: Why are we focused on the learning objectives *taxonomy* as opposed to simply focusing on learning objectives?

It's a good question considering that learning objectives are the most fundamentally important element of training design.

When many nontraining professionals are asked for their objectives, they often say things like "I'm going to talk about X topic," or "In the next 30 minutes, I'm going to cover six objectives." What they're really saying is that they have six talking points or their *own* goals for a session. True *learning* objectives are written in a *learner*-centric format, often completing some variation of "By the end of this session, the learners will be able to . . ."

Of course, there's no need to get into a debate with a SME about whether they're coming to you with true learning objectives or presentation goals and talking points. They don't really care what the nerdy, inside baseball definition of learning objectives may be. Our job is to translate their goals and talking points into true learning objectives that help accomplish the overall purpose of the learning program.

That said, it is absolutely essential that we, as learning professionals, are clear on what learning objectives are. Their purpose is to clearly and with specificity state what a *learner* should be able to do now or differently or better as the result of a training program. As long as you have the right learning objectives, your session can almost plan itself.

If you state that your learners will be able to *list* the five steps of your company's sales process, then you should logically have a component in which you introduce those five steps, and some sort of activity in which participants are tasked with recalling and listing those steps.

But what if you state that your learners will be able to *demonstrate* the five steps of your company's sales process? Changing that one verb means that your training program should look different. You'd still introduce the steps of the process, and perhaps you'll have a component in which participants need to recall and list those steps. However, if your objective is for learners to *demonstrate* those five steps, then you'll also need to be an activity in which participants practice using those five steps, probably with some sort of real-life simulation or role play.

With element 39, the words—and specifically the verbs—you choose, matter. Therein lies the "taxonomy" component. A taxonomy is a way of organizing and clustering concepts.

Perhaps the most well-known model for learning objectives taxonomy is Bloom's Taxonomy, which in its original form divides the intention behind your learning program into the following six categories from simplest to most complex:

- **Knowledge.** How can we get learners to know something? This aligns with objectives using verbs such as *define, list, identify,* or *describe.*
- **Comprehension.** How can we get learners to understand something? This aligns with objectives using verbs such as *compare, explain, describe,* or *infer.*
- **Application.** How can we get learners to use something? This aligns with objectives using verbs such as *demonstrate, use, create,* or *apply.*
- **Analysis.** How can we get learners to think critically about something? This aligns with objectives using verbs such as *analyze, differentiate, decide,* or *debate.*
- **Synthesis.** How can we get learners to put concepts together on their own? This aligns with objectives using verbs such as *hypothesize, integrate, revise,* or *plan.*
- **Evaluation.** How can we get learners to place value judgments on concepts? This aligns with objectives using verbs or phrases such as *assess, observe and provide peer feedback, perform a self-evaluation,* or *justify.*

Bloom's Taxonomy was revised in 2001, and the resulting Taxonomy for Teaching, Learning, and Assessment renamed the six categories to *remember, understand, apply, analyze, evaluate,* and *create.* There are a handful of other models for a learning objectives taxonomy as well. Keep in mind that all models are flawed, but some are useful if you understand the underlying principles of the model.

Using a learning objectives taxonomy can be extremely useful when mapping learning objectives to the business need of your learning program. If you simply want to generate awareness of a new policy or program without needing your learners to practice or develop corresponding skills, then drafting learning objectives from the knowledge or comprehension cluster may be adequate. If supervisors across your organization have identified a skills gap, an application-related learning objective would be appropriate. If you are training a group of new managers in a leadership development program, objectives that encourage synthesis and evaluation may be most appropriate.

Bonding your learning objectives taxonomy with the following elements may prove useful when deciding at which level your learners will be able to demonstrate successful completion of your program:

- **Soapbox (Sb).** Using this software tool, you'll be able to select from a list of prepared learning objectives. Once you decide which objectives are appropriate for your learning program, the software will generate a series of activities to help participants achieve those objectives.
- **Audience response (Re).** If you are satisfied with learning objectives at the knowledge or comprehension level, using audience response software can help you check for knowledge and understanding.
- **Quiz software (Qz).** Similar to audience response, you may choose to use game-like quiz software to put a different spin on the knowledge or understanding levels.
- **Dialogue education (De).** Due to the very nature of engaging in dialogue, the element of dialogue education will typically push training programs to "higher" levels along any taxonomy of learning objectives.
- **Lesson plan (Lp).** It's one thing to jot down a few learning objectives as you begin to plan a training program. Using a lesson plan can help ensure you connect specific talking points and activity instructions to each learning objective.
- **Microlearning (Mc).** Microlearning programs are, by their nature, extremely short. It's essential that you define exactly what someone should be able to do as a result, which can help keep the micro-experience tight, relevant, and effective.

Element 40
Instructional Design (Id)

Instructional design is the intentional process of deciding how (or if) training can help solve a problem, determining the best way to create a learning experience that will address the problem, and then evaluating the effectiveness of the learning experience. These are some core properties of instructional design:

- A structured approach
- A needs analysis, program design, and assessment (at a minimum)
- An engaging learning experience intended to meet an individual or organizational need

As with just about every other gas-like element on this periodic table, there are a variety of models that practitioners use for instructional design. Perhaps the most commonly used instructional design model is ADDIE:

- **Analysis.** What is the problem or challenge to be addressed and how do we know it's a problem or challenge?
- **Design.** What is the most effective way to deliver a learning experience that can address the problem or challenge?
- **Development.** How do we create the learning experience and who needs to be involved in the content development, activity development, and review of materials?
- **Implementation.** How, when, where, and with whom can we bring the learning experience to life?
- **Evaluation.** How effective was the learning experience?

While this model is sequential, it is also cyclical. In an ideal world, after you evaluate the learning experience, you'll return to the analysis phase to determine if there's still a need, and if so, if the design needs to be modified, and so on.

Using an instructional design model is important because it provides structure to the development of a learning experience. I have been approached too many times by someone who insists that training is necessary to address a problem or challenge. As an eager-to-please, early career training professional, I would jump right into the design phase as soon as someone came to me with a training request. If I had been more rigorous in applying any sort of instructional design model to my craft, I would have instead methodically begun with some sort of analysis to determine what the problem was and whether training was the right solution. There were times when I'd design a highly engaging program that didn't actually solve the problem, because it wasn't a training problem. I may have called myself an instructional designer at the time, but I was really more of an order taker.

As you explore the practice of instructional design, you may wish to bond it with any of these other elements:

- **Measuring for effectiveness (Me).** Regardless of the instructional design model that you choose to use, the final piece of the process will always involve evaluation, assessing, or measuring for effectiveness. The key is to include any sort of measurement into the design of the program so that it is a natural part of the learning experience and not simply an add-on after the fact.

- **Learning boosts (Lb).** One of the biggest challenges of looking at a two-dimensional visual representation of a model on paper or your computer screen is that it's easy to lose sight of the depth that goes into a process like instructional design. Steps such as design or implementation should not be thought of as one-time components. Incorporating an element such as learning boosts will mean that implementation is not a one-time event, but rather a series of pieces that make up a larger, more comprehensive learning experience.

- **Gamification (Gm).** You can learn a lot about people—the way they respond to pressure or adversity, work within a structured environment, adhere to rules, or choose to problem solve—through game play. Incorporating a string of game-based elements into the design of a learning experience can be a particularly useful strategy, as long as it aligns with the learning objectives that have been established to address a challenge or problem.

- **Learning objectives taxonomy (Lo).** As you've read earlier in this chapter, choosing the right learning objectives and connecting them to the appropriate learning activities is a core piece to any effective design step.

- **Data (Dt).** This element is a kind of alpha and omega when it comes to instructional design. Data will be an essential piece when kicking off an instructional design project and performing the initial assessment. Collecting good data during and following the implementation of a learning experience will be crucial when evaluating the effectiveness of the program.

Reflection: How Is Your Learning Program's Air Quality?

When gas-like elements are used appropriately, it's almost like you don't know they exist. When they're not present at all or when they are used poorly or too much, it can be hard to take in the content that's being shared during a learning program. Use Table 1-1 to determine the "air quality" of your learning programs. Are there elements that you need to use with more frequency? Are there times when certain elements are being overused or used poorly in combination with other elements? Are any elements being piped into your learning programs in an effective formula that should never be taken for granted or forgotten?

Then answer the question: What research, reading, training, or actions do I need to take to be able to pump more of these elements into my learning programs?

Table 1-1. Air Quality Monitor

	Poor Air Quality (There is a noticeable absence of these elements.)	Smoggy (These elements are overused.)	Clear (These elements seem to be used in the right proportion. I don't even notice them.)
Adult Learning (Al)			
Dialogue Education (De)			
Gamification (Gm)			
Change Management (Cm)			
Levels of Evaluation (Le)			
Visual Design (Vd)			
Learning Objectives Taxonomy (Lo)			
Instructional Design (Id)			

Chapter 2
Liquid Elements

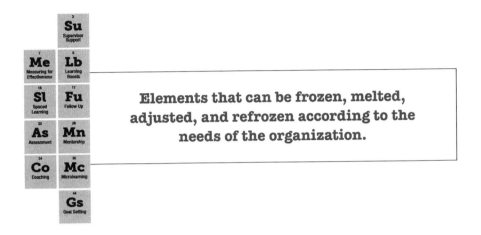

Elements that can be frozen, melted, adjusted, and refrozen according to the needs of the organization.

A number of years ago I became the director of training for a national nonprofit organization that worked in the foster care system. Specifically, our organization was responsible for providing materials to help recruit and train volunteers to go into a court case involving abuse and neglect, make a determination about what was in the best interest of the child, and make a recommendation to the judge. This was literally life-changing work for all involved, and the training needed to not only be high quality and engaging, the volunteers needed to retain as much information as possible.

Years before I came on board, the company had developed a 30-hour training program that was distributed to local nonprofit and government-based organizations across the country. It was broken down into three-hour segments and delivered in-person, typically over the course of 10 weeks.

When I started with this organization, I wanted to quickly put my mark on the training program; I scoured it to find weaknesses, ready to bring a fresh set of ideas to the program. Unfortunately for me (or better said, unfortunately for my ego), it turned out that the program was instructionally sound and really well designed. It was a model spaced-learning program, delivering three-hour chunks of content on a wide variety of topics, allowing participants to digest the information and even do homework between sessions, then asking them to build upon what they'd already learned with the next three-hour chunk of content.

However, after several years of talking with local programs across the country, it became clear that 30 hours of required, in-person training was a barrier to recruiting new volunteers. We brainstormed new training models and came up with a blended approach that would continue to fulfill the 30-hour training requirement while offering more flexibility to those volunteers with busier schedules.

While new curriculum still required periodic in-person check-ins (which included simulations and learning assessments) over the course of a month or more, volunteers were able to complete a large portion of their training online.

The point of my story is that liquid elements, a very important component of learning experiences, may be locked in place for years as they successfully meet an organization's needs, but they can and should be revisited and reassessed from time to time to ask the question: Are we doing things the same way because they're meeting our needs, or are we doing things the same way because it's convenient and the way we've always done them?

What Are Liquid Elements?

The 10 liquid elements are supervisor support (Su), measuring for effectiveness (Me), learning boosts (Lb), spaced learning (Sl), follow up (Fu), assessment (As), mentorship (Mn), coaching (Co), microlearning (Mc), and goal setting (Gs). They share three properties:

- They are practices designed to support knowledge and skill transfer.
- They take the shape of the vessel (usually the organization or the team) into which they are poured.
- They can be frozen and locked into place as needed, then melted so that the shape can change and be adjusted, as appropriate.

The way in which you use liquid elements and the degree to which they can be effective will depend on your organizational culture, learners, and management buy-in.

Many organizations still rely overwhelmingly on formal training—whether classroom, virtual, or e-learning—to address employee learning needs. Pouring one or more of these liquid elements, such as learning boosts (Lb), spaced learning (Sl), or microlearning (Mc), offers a way to unfreeze an organization's this-is-the-way-we've-always-done-things mentality to make an overall learning program more effective.

Combining those with formal learning programs can create a mixture of foundational knowledge (through classroom training) and ongoing informational nuggets that lead to higher retention and on-the-job application. With microlearning pieces, such as short stories or video clips distributed prior to a training session, talent development professionals can prime learners' minds. Providing additional pieces of content—such as short articles, quizzes, action plans, or job aids—as part of a learning boost initiative after employees complete a session or e-learning module can go a long way in aiding retention.

No matter how amazing your training design or engaging your delivery, people will forget things as time passes between when they first learned your content and when they need to try to recall it. This is known as the forgetting curve (Figure 2-1). According to Art Kohn, a professor at the Portland State University School of Business who has written extensively on the connection between brain science and the implications for learning, "If you provide your learners with booster events in the hours and days after training, you can reshape their forgetting curve. For example, if you provide employees with a leadership seminar on Monday, you can expect that most of this information will be lost within a week. However, if you provide a booster event, such as a multiple-choice questionnaire, it causes the learner to recall the information, which will reset the learner's forgetting curve."

Figure 2-1. The Forgetting Curve

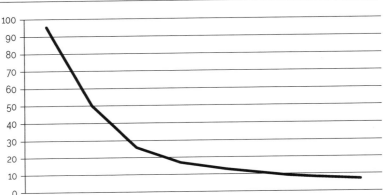

Time is represented from left to right. Left is shortly after learning. Right is long after learning.

Source: Thalheimer (2010), worklearning.com.

Finding ways to integrate these liquid elements to boost learner retention and make on-the-job application more likely may require melting the old, frozen organizational learning habits down into a more fluid set of practices.

Liquid elements go beyond techniques to help with retention. A wide variety of learner-centered practices, such as follow-up (Fu), supervisor support (Su), and performance-based goal setting (Gs), are also essential to employees simply understanding why they need to continue learning and improving in the first place.

Sometimes once you've melted down practices you can mix them with new elements and refreeze—that is, codify them into organizational practices and culture. There are other times when it's best to leave practices fluid and allow them to ebb and flow as situations warrant.

We're now going to take a closer look at the 10 liquid elements, how you might encounter them in the workplace, and the variety of ways you can implement them.

Element 2
Supervisor Support (Su)

Supervisor support, in the context of the elements of effective learning experiences, refers to the way in which a people manager helps learners get better at their jobs. The "supervisor" in this element refers to the immediate manager of a learner.

While different supervisors will have different approaches to people management, some primary properties of this element that influence training experiences include:

- The supervisor provides specific feedback to the learner on current performance or needed skills.
- The supervisor sets performance goals with the learner.
- The supervisor identifies ways for the learner to meet performance gaps.
- The supervisor holds the learner accountable for performance.

The gazillion dollar question is: What in the world does a person's supervisor have to do with effective learning experiences, especially if they'll rarely (if ever) be in the same training room as the learner?

The answer is: A lot!

In their book *Transfer of Training*, Mary Broad and John Newstrom conclude that whether or not information or skills from a learning experience are applied on the job depends on a person's supervisor, both before and after the learning experience. If you think about it, it makes a lot of sense. Wouldn't you be more apt to put something to use if you sat down with your supervisor in advance of a training program to identify specific skills gaps or learning needs and set a goal for how that course can help meet your needs? Wouldn't you try harder to apply what you've learned if, after you completed a training course, your supervisor asked: Can I see what you're doing that's new or different or better?

So how do we take advantage of supervisor support if supervisors are not really in our audience? My simple answer is that supervisors *should* be part of our audience. Not the primary audience, of course; supervisors are not typically going through the learning experience *with* the learners. But they are stakeholders and perhaps secondary audience members.

You can leverage supervisor support by bonding the following elements to a training program:

- **Handouts (Hn).** Perhaps the most common way for training designers to engage their learners' supervisors is through handouts, self-assessment forms, or action plans that are shared with supervisors once a training program has been completed. I've seen some training programs go so far as to mail carbonless or photocopied action plans to a learner's supervisor.

- **Follow up (Fu).** Sending a survey to your learners' supervisors at some point 30 to 90 days following the conclusion of your training program could help prompt a follow-up conversation between supervisors and those who completed the program. Follow-up surveys also help you collect Level 3 data (transfer to the job) that is not self-reported by your learners, but rather an outside observer (their supervisor).

- **Text tools (Tt).** If you've secured permission to send text message reminders to the supervisors of your learners, you can automate goal setting and discussion prompts that will help managers engage their direct reports in targeted conversations. Without such prompts, some supervisors may want to support and follow up with your learners, but may not know enough about the training program to have a productive conversation.

- **Data (Dt).** Pre- and post-test information, narrative observations, or activity results are all data that could be shared with supervisors to let them know how a learner progressed through a training program. If you're designing e-learning content, this data can be generated fairly easily through your LMS. For instructor-led courses, collecting data can be more challenging, but if it's part of the initial course design (and not something you decide to do at the last minute), then you can offer some valuable insights to managers.
- **Goal setting (Gs).** Some training programs have extensive pre-work, including the required completion of 360-degree feedback instruments and information on how to sit down with a supervisor to set goals based on the results of that feedback and the learning program's objectives.

Ask the next 10 people you see whether they've ever had a supervisor follow up with them about a training program they've been through; the results may be discouraging. There are several reasons why this element may be so fluid:

- **Priority of the training program.** Very few organizations want their employees to go offline with their daily duties to spend time in training. If a supervisor doesn't buy in to the value of your training program, chances for their support are slim. A number of conferences now have a specific area on their websites to help you convince your supervisor why attending will bring value to attendees, their teams, and their organizations. Don't forget that when you're creating a training program, you're not only an instructional designer—you're also a marketer. Be sure the value your training program offers to participants, their teams, and their organizations is clear in any communication you share.
- **Experience level of the supervisor.** A survey from workplace learning company Grovo in 2016 revealed that 98 percent of managers felt that managers within their company "needed more training to deal with important issues such as professional development, conflict resolution, employee turnover, time management, and project management." Some managers, especially those new to their role as a supervisor, simply don't know how to manage and support their direct reports, or they may assume that the burden should fall on learners to take control over their own

performance improvement. Offering guides, handouts, or electronic communication to participants' supervisors may help equip those managers with tools they didn't even know they needed.

- **Supervisor's available time.** People managers are busy. Some are also "working managers," meaning they need to balance developing their direct reports with moving their own work forward. Some are senior managers or executives responsible for teams or divisions. Checklists or check-in discussion prompts that participants can share with their managers could make supervisor support easier on everyone.
- **Organizational culture.** Some organizations invest a lot of time in developing their people managers, while others may believe they hire the right people and expect them to take control over their own performance. If you are an internal training resource developing programs for your organization, finding champions within the organization who buy in to the concept of supervisor support may be one (slow but sure) way to gently shift the culture. If you're an external training developer, you'll need to rely on communication, marketing, and intentionally including the concept of supervisor support into the programs you develop.

Element 7
Measuring for Effectiveness (Me)

With measuring for effectiveness, you are gauging the impact of a learning experience against the intended outcomes.

Some of the primary properties of this element include:

- A baseline has been established
- One or more measurement instruments are used
- Outside factors are controlled for (to the fullest extent possible)
- Answers the question: Would people have been better off if this training program didn't exist?

The tricky thing about trying to measure any training program for effectiveness is that there are so many other variables that could influence the results. Is a boost in sales following a training program the result of a sales team who is now better equipped and more knowledgeable, or is it the result of a strong overall economy? Is increased retention and job satisfaction the result of a new coaching program, or are employees simply happier because the weather has turned nicer? There are a lot of factors at play and very few (if any) organizations are willing to invest the time, money, and resources needed for a scientific study of the impact or effectiveness or a training program.

That said, learning professionals still shouldn't disregard the need to measure whether or not a learning program was effective. After all, why should your organization bother to allocate money for learning programs? Why should employees bother logging into the LMS to access your e-learning library or attending your next session on leadership development?

Bonding the following elements with measuring for effectiveness can be a way to get a clearer picture of whether the program you've put together is effective:

- **Smile sheets (Sm).** While good post-training evaluations don't guarantee learning happened, poor post-training evaluations often indicate that learning probably didn't happen. There's only so much useful information (when it comes to measuring training effectiveness) that can be gleaned from smile sheets, but they do offer one data point by providing insight into your learners' reactions to the learning experience.

- **Assessment (As).** You can examine participants' increase in knowledge or skills using the activities that take place during or following a learning experience through post-testing or on-the-job observation. Again, no single measurement instrument will give you all the information you need to know, but having multiple data points allows you to put together a story about the effectiveness (or lack thereof) of your learning experience.

- **Levels of evaluation (Le).** Working your way up the four levels of evaluation, you can collect data points that paint a clearer picture of your program's effectiveness by gauging learner reaction, knowledge, transfer to the job, and on-the-job results.

- **Instructional design (Id).** You can't wait to plan measurement until after your boss says: "You know that training program you launched three months ago? Do we know if it was effective at all?" If you're going to try to measure the effectiveness, then you'll want to bake that measurement into the original program design, beginning with assessing for the needs you're going to fill and determining the program's learning objectives.

- **Role play (Rp).** While role play and simulation activities are done in the relative safety and security of the training environment, observing changes in participant behavior and knowledge during these activities can offer preliminary information on whether you can reasonably expect to see real world results.
- **Data (Dt).** Every single suggested element to bond with measuring for effectiveness has provided a way to collect data. Data—both qualitative and quantitative—offers insight into the impact and effectiveness of a training program. Some programs such as team building may not need many data points, while other programs such as executive coaching or sales training may require a variety of data points and a longer period to gauge effectiveness.

As you look to measure for effectiveness, there are several variables you'll want to account for:

- **Lack of a baseline for comparative purposes.** How can you know that something is effective unless you have a point of comparison? Being able to collect baseline data against which you can compare the performance of those who have gone through your training program can help determine if the program had an impact or if people truly were better off without it.
- **Outside factors.** There will always be factors outside the control of your instructional design and facilitation skills. Things such as the economy, company culture, workload of your participants, language or culture barriers, technological savvy, and even things like a participant's (or their boss's) mood after the Super Bowl, can all have an impact on the effectiveness of your training program.
- **Time.** Humans adopt new practices and behaviors at very different speeds. It's possible that measuring a program's effectiveness after three months could yield results that are very different than if you measured a year after the program concludes.
- **Subjective data.** The type of data you collect and how you collect it will go a long way in determining if it paints an objective picture of your program's results. Are you relying primarily on self-reported information? People tend to think more highly of their own performance. Does anyone have incentive to paint a rosier (or bleaker) picture of the impact of the training? Sometimes in an

effort to prove something we want to be true (that our training program was super effective, for example), we look for data that supports our case while ignoring or not collecting data that suggests otherwise.

Element 8
Learning Boosts (Lb)

No matter how important your content, how creative your design, or how engaging your delivery, people will forget things. They'll forget important things. Unless they get a little nudge.

Enter the learning boost.

Learning boosts are bits of information, content, or even a quiz question sent to learners after a learning experience that force them to retrieve information and to help keep the content accessible in their short-term memory bank. In short, learning boosts are designed to help your learners forget less of your content and transform more of it into knowledge and actions that come increasingly instinctively. Learning boosts should be brief and focus exclusively on content already covered.

Perhaps you've watched a gameshow or you've been playing a knowledge-based game like *Trivial Pursuit*, and you hear a question that makes you think: "Once upon a time I knew the answer to that . . . it's on the tip of my tongue . . . give me a minute . . . meh, I don't remember . . . what's the answer?" Then you hear the answer and you swear you'll never forget it again as long as you live.

That's a bit like how learning boosts work. With a learning boost, you expose your participants to previously covered information, content, and skills so that they have to search their memory and recall what they once learned. The best part is that the boosts don't need to be very long. Art Kohn (2014), the brain science researcher mentioned earlier, described a recent study that seemed to advocate for short boosts. "The testers gave one group of learners a five-second booster experience, the second group got a 30-second booster experience, and the third group got a five-minute booster experience. All were later tested for their recall and you know what? There was no difference between the groups! The group whose boost lasted only five seconds did just as well as the other two groups."

Learning boosts can come in a variety of forms, and bonding them with the following elements can maximize their effectiveness:

- **Spaced learning (Sl).** Learning boosts aren't simply something to send out after a training program has concluded. Multipart learning experiences—whether asynchronous online courses or multiday or multiweek in-person training programs—can integrate short quizzes and boost previous learning before moving on to new content.
- **Follow up (Fu).** This can take the form of supervisor support or messaging from you to your participants after a course has been completed. Instead of allowing a certificate of completion to be the final thing your participants experience, sending periodic communications (and quizzes) or providing collateral for participants to use with their supervisors can assist in boosting post-course retention.
- **Instructional design (Id).** Learning boosts can't be an afterthought or something trendy to stick at the end of a course on a whim. Careful planning about what would be most valuable to reinforce, as well as how and when to reinforce it, are key considerations that need to be baked into your course design.
- **Text tools (Tt).** People typically leave text messages unopened much less frequently than they leave emails unopened. In that sense, text messaging can be a very effective way to communicate with participants following a course. There are a variety of tools on the market to help set up short, text-based quizzes or information nuggets that are sent automatically at a cadence that works for your program.
- **Email (Em).** People expect to get work-related emails and, like text tools, there are a variety of email-based tools you can use to automatically distribute short videos, bursts of information, job aids, polls, or quizzes to help remind your participants about the most important aspects of your course.

Reasons learning boosts fluid:

- **"I'm an adult and I can study the stuff I need on my own."** Once people finish school, they can have a natural resentment toward jumping through anyone else's hoops or taking a test. They may think that being a professional means you can be responsible for your own success—and while you remember the important things for your job, if you wanted to recall something you could just study it on your own. You don't need to be tested, especially after a course has completed. Unfortunately, research doesn't support the effectiveness of this perception. In their book *Make It Stick: The Science of Successful Learning*, Peter Brown, Henry Roediger III, and Mark McDaniel offer a wide variety of studies on the importance of formal learning boosts. "In one experiment college students studied prose passages on various scientific topics like those taught in college and then either took an immediate recall test after initial exposure or restudied the material. After a delay of two days, the students who took the initial test recalled more of the material than those who simply restudied it (68 v. 54 percent) and this advantage was sustained a week later (56 v. 42 percent). Another experiment found that after one week a study-only group showed the most forgetting of what they initially had been able to recall, forgetting 52 percent, compared to a repeated-testing group, who forgot only 10 percent."

- **Reluctance to give contact information.** Employment laws, company culture, and personal boundaries can influence how you roll out a learning boost system. Sending work-related tasks to hourly employees using text or email could fall outside their employment agreements. Using email or text messaging (which is still considered a personal form of communication) may also go against company culture or garner pushback from employees, especially if learning boosts are sent to personal devices. Securing permission from the organization (and often individual learners) will be an important step toward the success of a learning boost initiative.

- **Lack of accountability.** It's easy for someone to just hit delete or let a boost fall to the bottom of their inbox if they think they've completed a course and it's no longer a priority.

- **Perceived as trivia.** There's a fine line between boosting knowledge and spamming people with trivia. Ensuring participants know they will be receiving post-course communication intended to help their retention and ultimately improve their performance can be a useful step in implementation. Learners always want to know "what's in it for me?" whether you're doing an activity during a learning program or sending follow-up messaging.

Element 16
Spaced Learning (Sl)

Learning and development expert Mike Taylor has spent a lot of time studying what the field of corporate training can learn (and steal) from the advertising industry. "No company has ever just run one ad on one day, and then never advertised again. If you pay attention to how companies advertise, it's more of a drip campaign in which you may see a billboard, you may hear an ad on the radio, see a commercial on tv, see a sponsorship of a local youth sports team. This is something that the world of L&D can really learn from" (Washburn 2020).

In other words, it can behoove training program designers to spread learning out over time. This concept, also known as spaced learning, has several distinct properties:

- There is more than one learning "touch point"
- It includes a pause between when content or skills are taught
- Content or skills are revisited following the pause

Spaced learning can take many forms—from a year-long leadership development program for high-potential managers to an asynchronous, online course offering a certification in project management. Offering space between learning experiences can allow participants to go back to their desks, try out your concepts, have some real-world experience, and return to the next learning experience with thoughts, questions, or reflections that make your content more memorable and real.

Beyond a simple lesson to be learned from the advertising industry, data supports the effectiveness of spaced learning in improving learner retention, and if your learners aren't *remembering* your content, they'll never be able to *use* it.

Will Thalheimer, in the 2006 report *Spaced Learning Events Over Time: What the Research Says*, examined more than 100 research articles on the topic and concluded that "spacing learning over time produces substantial learning benefits. . . . Spaced-repetition effects are particularly noteworthy given the enormous research literature supporting their use." A flood of research, articles, and books published since then continue to support the importance of spaced learning.

In their 2020 book, *Evidence-Informed Learning Design: Creating Training to Improve Performance*, Mirjam Neelen and Paul Kirschner cite various studies and conclude that "tackling whatever we need to learn in various ways promotes remembering and applying knowledge and skills because we have 'recorded' it in a slightly different way each time and this makes our knowledge and/or skills more flexible. Although it might seem that spaced learning takes more time, and this might be the case in the short term, it actually improves our learning and we'll remember what we've learned a lot longer."

A variety of methods for spaced learning can emerge when this element is bonded with one or more of the following elements:

- **E-learning (El).** Breaking longer courses (I've been involved in the development of courses that can run an hour or more!) down into shorter, 15-minute chunks with a review of what was learned in previous chunks may be one way to go. Multiweek, asynchronous online courses during which participants can be exposed to content and do assignments at their own pace may also be a way to space out the learning and revisit key points.
- **Microlearning (Mc).** In addition to short e-learning modules, you can design short videos, articles, or tutorials into your spaced cadence of content to reinforce previously covered concepts.
- **Instructional design (Id).** Like many other elements, spaced learning isn't something to throw together at the last minute. It needs to be intentionally designed whether you're developing instructor-led or online learning experiences, presenting content, or pausing that content and returning to it later in the session or during a second or third session down the road.
- **Email (Em).** Similar to the way in which learning boosts operate, sending automated emails with bits of content or short quizzes can help learners revisit and recall key information.

Despite how powerful supporting research for spaced learning is, there will be those in your organization who want to "just get it over with." Element 16 may be met with skepticism by some decision makers, turning up the heat so high on the concept that this entire liquid element is at risk of evaporating. There's a school of thought that suggests it's better to just sit through a full-day session and get it over with as opposed to needing to attend a series of three 2-hour sessions that take place over the course of one month. This can be a difficult balance to strike because while *some* learning experience may be better than no learning experience at all, there is clear evidence that retention (and therefore the propensity to use what's learned) goes up when learning is spaced. If multiple sessions won't work, using text tools or emails to follow up and offer learning boosts may be the most practical way to go.

Element 17
Follow Up (Fu)

The training program is over. . . . now what?

When this question was posed at SightLife—the world's largest eye bank providing sight-restoring corneal transplants in an effort to eliminate corneal blindness worldwide—they chose to distribute certificates to all doctors in their training program only after they completed one last piece of homework. The doctors had to return to their practices and share (via email to the training coordinator) how the training program influenced their work with the next several patients that they saw.

The element of follow up can be characterized by asking, "How will the learners be held accountable to put the investment that's made in their professional development—in terms of time and money—into action?"

Follow up often includes post-training communication or assignments as well as transfer support of training from the training environment to the real world. It can come in many forms, from action plans completed during a session then shared with a supervisor to post-training email reminders about key content to homework assignments that need to be submitted before receiving a certificate of completion.

Whichever form seems most appropriate to your context, here are a few reasons why some sort of follow up is an essential element to any training program you hope will be effective:

- **Is training technically complete if it's not tried in the real world?** When it comes to doing new things, there's always a first time and that first time is often uncomfortable. It can simply be easier to revert to the old, comfortable ways of doing things. Find a follow up strategy that supports learners in applying what they've learned in the real world, ideally with a feedback or support mechanism so they can reflect on their first attempt and make corrections as necessary.
- **People forget a lot of what they've learned.** Regardless of how amazing a learning experience you've created, the forgetting curve

is something you'll be fighting against. Providing a post-training support mechanism can help your learners actively want to remember what they've learned.

- **Outside the training environment, employees are busy.** While terms like *learners* and *participants* have been woven throughout this book, neither are actually job titles. When it comes to training programs, we're developing them for employees who have a lot of demands on their time. When they have completed a training program, they still have phone calls and emails and fires to put out. Follow up can help make sure they take some time out to recall their training amid everything else they have going on.

Follow up is a sneaky-important element to effective training. While it's tempting to think that a training program concludes at the end of the final day of an instructor-led session or with the last screen of an e-learning program, that doesn't quite do justice to an initiative you want people to remember and apply on the job. When you look at the rest of the periodic table, there are a number of elements that can be bonded with follow up to meet the needs of your organization:

- **Supervisor support (Su).** An employee's supervisor is the most important factor when it comes to predicting whether someone will apply new knowledge, skills, or abilities to the job. Ensuring supervisors are seen as stakeholders in any training design and providing checklists, action plans, or other tools to help them support their employees after a training program can make a big difference.

- **Learning boosts (Lb).** Providing opportunities for learners to recall information after a training program has been completed through the strategic, timely distribution of short quiz questions or nuggets of information to supplement what was learned can help keep your content front-of-mind.

- **Handouts (Hn).** Whether you've provided an entire participant guide, standalone job aids, or action plans, giving participants something tangible to walk away with can help them return to your content in their time of need. Participants can mark key information in the documents, which will help them act independently and recall it long after a training program has been completed.

- **Spaced learning (Sl).** Multipart courses that take place over a period of time offer a natural opportunity to check in on how prior content has been applied before moving on to new material
- **Change management (Cm).** Most learning and development initiatives revolve around some sort of change—change in behaviors, change in performance, change in culture—and no change comes about through a single event. Creating sustainable change requires effort, consistency, and follow up.
- **Microlearning (Mc).** Follow up doesn't need to be complicated. Providing brief snippets of information, videos, or short e-learning modules as a way to supplement the content that was provided and keep the learning going can offer simple opportunities for learners to continue to grow and apply new skills.
- **Goal setting (Gs).** Giving learners an opportunity to set goals for themselves (ideally in conversation with their supervisor) in advance of participating in a learning program can be an extremely helpful strategy to ensure they understand why they're participating and what they hope to get out of the course. Referencing these goals after a training program can make any follow up initiative more relevant.

Element 25
Assessment (As)

"That was the best training I've ever attended!"

That's one of the most popular siren songs ever offered to training professionals. (If you're unfamiliar with a "siren song," *Merriam Webster* defines it as "an alluring utterance or appeal, especially one that is seductive or deceptive.")

We all want to be liked, adored even. We want to be told our work is amazing. When it comes to training programs, comments like this are certainly nice to hear. (I won't ever argue with someone who shares this feedback with me!) The more important question, however, is, how do we know the program was effective? For the answer, we need to adopt the element of assessment.

Assessment is an attempt to determine the effectiveness of a learning initiative and has the following core properties:

- It may involve qualitative or quantitative measures
- It is targeted to provide a snapshot of whether learning objectives have been accomplished

The element of assessment can be an extremely broad concept and can include all sorts of methods, from formal quizzes or certification exams to informal participant observations or quiz games like *Jeopardy*.

Perhaps the best way to explore the variety of assessments that can be used to help determine the effectiveness of your training initiative is by taking a look at how to bond other elements into them:

- **Audience response (Re).** Using real-time audience response activities to poll your participants can help you determine their prior knowledge of a subject or it can give you insights into how much they have learned, depending on the timing of the activity. Keep in mind that polling your audience is a "soft" measure that is often done anonymously to provide an overall trend of where your participants stand, but it is often difficult to use polling data to assess the learning or skill development of individuals.

- **Quiz software (Qz).** Using quiz software allows you to assess how much individuals or groups have learned, often in a fun (sometimes competitive) way. Whether you're using an online platform such as Kahoot or you've created a *Jeopardy*-like game using PowerPoint, quizzing your participants allows you to take a snapshot of knowledge learned at a given point in your session. While knowledge checks alone may not give you the entire picture of overall program effectiveness, they do offer some data on whether participants are growing their knowledge base.

- **Levels of evaluation (Le).** In addition to capturing comments such as "best training ever" and "room was too cold," post-training evaluation forms can offer participant reactions on how confident they are as they complete your training program and set out to use new knowledge or skills in the real world. Pre- and post-testing can offer you some insights as to whether new knowledge was gained, although the asterisk with this measure is that post-tests are often conducted right after participants have learned a concept. The forgetting curve can wreak havoc on post-test results, so if you really want to assess training effectiveness in terms of knowledge gained using post-testing, you should wait a week to administer the test. Gathering information about participants post-training performance and transfer of skills onto the job can provide insight into on-the-job effectiveness if you survey participants (or their supervisors) 30 or 60 days after the program has been completed.

- **E-learning (El).** On the surface this may be an odd element to bond with assessment since e-learning is typically thought of as a training method or even distribution channel for dispersed groups of learners. However, e-learning can hold a natural assessment advantage over other forms of training delivery because many LMSs capture all sorts of data that can be used to assess the effectiveness of the program. The key here is building those means of assessment into the design of the course and then ensuring your LMS can capture the data you want.

- **Instructional design (Id).** This has and will be said many times throughout this book, but I have no qualms about repeating myself on this point. If you're planning to assess the effectiveness of a training program, it needs to be baked into the design of the program from the beginning. What baseline data will you capture in your needs assessment to help you answer the question, "Why are we doing this training and how will we know it's effective?" Using well-crafted learning objectives will help you design activities and assessment strategies to determine the effectiveness of your program.

- **Role play (Rp).** While many participants will groan at the mention of role play, if it is designed well this element can offer key insights into whether your participants can say the right words and react in an appropriate manner during a real-life simulation.

- **Games (Ga).** Quiz games offer insights into knowledge gain. Inspiration can also be drawn from role-playing games or escape room–type activities in which individuals or small groups need to debate the merits of their decisions in order to proceed through the game, which offers greater insights into critical thinking, decision making, and teamwork.

If you're just looking for an at-a-glance list of potential assessment activities, here are some ideas:

- Polls
- Quizzes
- Knowledge check–style games inspired by things like *Jeopardy*, *Family Feud*, or *Trivial Pursuit*

- Critical thinking–type games inspired by *Dungeons and Dragons*, *Pandemic*, or activities like escape or puzzle rooms
- Role play
- Case studies
- Small-group discussion
- Large-group discussion
- Individual reflections or journaling
- Debate
- Individual practicum (a challenge in which individuals need to demonstrate they've achieved competence in a given skill)
- Participant-led teach backs
- Post-training evaluation
- Post-training survey sent to participants or supervisors
- Comparing individual or organizational KPIs prior to and following training program

Element 26
Mentorship (Mn)

As I mentioned to start the previous chapter, when I took a job as a GED instructor, I wanted to do right by every young adult I was teaching, but I didn't have a clue how to develop lesson plans, much less an entire curriculum. My father, a former staff development specialist at his public school, entered the picture and led me through an informal crash course on instructional design. To this day we'll continue to bounce ideas around when I get stuck.

While I eventually took several masters-level courses on instructional design, when I was a GED instructor I didn't have the time or the money for formal training on the topic. My father's mentorship got me to a "good enough" place to develop an entire GED curriculum that helped dozens of my students earn their high school equivalency credential.

There is always someone smarter or more experienced from whom you can learn. Perhaps they work within your organization, perhaps they're part of an industry trade group to which you also belong, or perhaps it's a family member, a friend, or just someone you see from time to time. These mentors can offer a lifetime of lessons learned—quickly, informally, and oftentimes for the price of a cup of coffee (and maybe a pastry).

A mentoring relationship can be either formal (many organizations have programs to match less experienced employees with someone who has experience or expertise in a particular area) or informal (think of someone you meet regularly for coffee to discuss issues at work).

Here are two core properties of mentorship:

- A supportive relationship
- At least one person in the relationship has experience or knowledge in a specific area

While mentorship and the element coaching (Co) are sometimes used interchangeably, there are some clear distinctions between these two elements, as highlighted in Table 2-1.

Table 2-1. Mentoring Versus Coaching

Mentorship	Coaching
• Can be formal (employer-sponsored) or informal (periodic networking meetups with someone in the industry) • Conversations typically have a general direction: specific outcomes may or may not be part of the expectation • Mentors often serve as a guide and cheerleader, but accountability (if present) typically resides with the mentee	• A formal relationship • Clear outcomes • Conversations generally follow a structure or model • Coach generally takes responsibility for holding someone accountable

When you think of the benefits of mentorship, such as personal support, a greater feeling of connection, access to expertise, and immediate access to knowledge or experience, there are many ways to enhance learning programs using this element. There are several scenarios in which mentorship can be extremely beneficial:

- **Being new to the organization.** In addition to a formal onboarding process, pairing new employees with someone in their department can enhance their understanding of organizational culture as well as how they fit into the organization. (It may be even better to pair them with someone outside their department so they can be exposed to different roles and perspectives.) No new employee onboarding program can cover everything, but the strategic use of mentors for new employees can offer insights and deeper connections to the organization than a formal training program can provide.

- **Transitioning from individual contributor to manager.** This is perhaps the biggest leap someone can take in their career, and without adequate support, it can be a very rough experience. Connecting new managers with people who have been there can help make that leap less scary, less lonely, and more successful.

- **Grooming a high-potential leader.** How do leaders in the organization communicate? How should executive presentations be put together? Answers to questions like these may not be instinctive. It's one thing to go from individual contributor to manager, but making the leap into the executive ranks is a whole other world. While leadership development courses or MBA programs may offer critical formal learning opportunities, there is no substitute for having an ongoing, supportive relationship with someone who can guide you through the highs and lows of breaking into the executive level of an organization.

The incorporation of an informal learning strategy of mentorship into your initiatives can be strengthened with bonds to one or more of the following elements:

- **Subject matter experts (Ex).** People who have expertise in their field can offer a lot when given an opportunity to enter into a supportive relationship with those hungry for their knowledge. While SMEs may not have a lot of time to offer, time spent in a mentoring relationship truly is quality over quantity.

- **Spaced learning (Sl).** Whether it's connected to new employee onboarding or some other training program, using mentors to follow up with training participants in a periodic, ongoing manner can help keep the learning fresh and offer participants an opportunity to ask questions and reflect on experiences after they've returned to their desk and tried things out in the real world.

- **Virtual meeting (Vm).** PATH, a global health organization headquartered in Seattle, recently overhauled a training program that was once held completely in person. With the program transitioning to an online environment, the creators were concerned that the participants (who are dispersed in field offices around the world) wouldn't have a connection to a real person. PATH chose to incorporate a virtual mentorship program in which experienced staff would use a virtual meeting platform to connect with trainees, answer their questions, and simply let them know that they weren't working in isolation.

- **Instructional design (Id).** If mentorship is going to be part of a formal learning program, then it needs to have an intentional design. Beyond the mere idea of incorporating mentors into a program, you'll have to identify the mentors, make sure they are adequately prepared and have clarity around what they're expected to do, and ensure their mentor meetings are a productive use of everyone's time.
- **Goal setting (Gs).** Is mentorship intended to create greater connection among employees? Is it intended to reduce the amount of time employees spend in a formal training program? The goals for any sort of mentorship need to be clearly defined to make sure it's an effective element in your learning program.

Element 34
Coaching (Co)

The term "coaching" can evoke a lot of emotions for a lot of people. Some don't like the concept because of a poor experience they had with a high school or college athletic coach who pushed them too far. Some may recoil at the concept because when they are referred for "coaching" at their company it means they're being taken into their supervisor's office for remediation or discipline.

In the context of our periodic table, and in an effort to maximize the effectiveness of learning experiences, the element coaching is very different from these experiences. Coaching is a supportive relationship in which the coach serves as a guide, offering structure to a coachee, with the belief that the coachee will be able to identify solutions to their own challenges.

Key properties of the coaching element include:
- One-on-one relationship
- Structured conversations at a regular interval
- Specific goals are identified
- Coach provides guidance, not answers

The ultimate goals for coaching include personal growth and professional development; it can be a powerful supplement to formal training programs. Some areas a coach focuses on are simple and straightforward, which allows a productive resolution to arrive quickly. In many areas, however, a coaching relationship will be ongoing as the coach and coachee engage in conversations that require focus and patience. With this in mind, there are some instances in which coaching is appropriate, but other situations in which it should absolutely not be incorporated into a learning program (Table 2-2).

Table 2-2. When and When Not to Use Coaching

When to Use Coaching	When Not to Use Coaching
• As a structured follow-up to training programs • When an employee has a specific professional development need and a training program is not available or feasible • During one-on-one conversations between an employee and a supervisor	• When time is of the essence, particularly in emergency situations • When a solution to a performance gap is an organizational policy or procedure as opposed to an adaptive challenge • When the performance gap is the result of a lack of knowledge

Also, keep in mind that while coaching may bring about deeper-level conversations, it should never be confused with counseling or therapy.

In creating a bond between coaching and the following elements, you may find ways to strengthen the effectiveness of both technical and soft skill training initiatives:

- **Supervisor support (Su).** If supervisors have been adequately trained in proper coaching techniques (which often means they're using a specific coaching model), they can super-charge the impact of a learning program through additional, structured conversations. Coaching can also change the dynamic between an employee and their boss, taking a relationship in which the boss is expected to give answers to one in which the boss serves as a sort of guide on the side, empowering direct reports to find their own solutions while continuing to hold them accountable for results.
- **Spaced learning (Sl).** Whether the coach turns out to be a supervisor, another internal resource, or someone contracted from outside the organization, providing ongoing coaching following a learning experience will encourage the participant to recall content and skills learned and use them during discussions or coaching-based assignments.
- **Virtual meeting (Vm).** The best person to take on a coaching role may be located in another office that is half a world away. Leveraging

technology such as virtual meeting platforms so participants are able to engage with the most appropriate coach can be something to consider as you're designing your program.

- **Goal setting (Gs).** Pairing someone up for coaching will only yield results if the conversations are focused. Identifying and setting goals to be achieved during each coaching encounter is fundamental to a productive and narrowly targeted interaction.

Element 35
Microlearning (Mc)

Have you ever looked up a YouTube video to figure out how to do a home improvement project (or how to assemble a toy on Christmas Eve when you couldn't decipher the instructions that came in the box)? Chances are you found what you were looking for in the form of a five(ish)-minute video. This is an example of microlearning, which is an element whose properties include:

- Short bursts of content
- Narrowly focused
- Available in the moment of need

Some people will ask, "Well, how long can something be and still be considered microlearning?" The truth is that there is no hard and fast rule—there isn't an International Federation of Microlearning that can officially accredit microlearning content based on its duration. As its name implies, it's intended to be micro, so if you put together a 10-minute resource—be it a job aid, video, or e-learning course—and choose to call it microlearning, it may not be as "micro" as some people expect.

I don't know of any effective training programs designed to help someone master a skill that consists 100 percent of microlearning bursts. Many people find standalone microlearning content to be extremely convenient and useful as an informal just-in-time job aid or refresher. Other learning teams integrate short microlearning bursts with other more formal learning approaches, such as an instructor-led or e-learning course.

While microlearning itself is simply a concept, it can be bonded with the following elements to be extremely impactful:

- **Learning boosts (Lb).** Microlearning through post-training learning boosts can be an important strategy to aid retention and keep content front-of-mind for your learners.

- **Video (Vi).** Tutorials, screencasts, animations, or recordings of thought leaders sharing their perspectives may be all an employee needs to quickly learn a concept or shortcut or be reminded of something they once had learned.
- **Rapid authoring (Ra).** Tools like Adobe Captivate or Articulate Storyline are often used for developing full-blown e-learning modules, but they also can (and should) be used to create small nuggets of information that don't need to be extensive or tracked in an LMS. They just need to be available to employees on-demand.
- **Collaborative file sharing (Cf).** Microlearning doesn't need to take a lot of time or effort to develop. Making job aids, policy summaries, diagrams, flow charts, or other tools and documentation easily accessible through a central repository like Sharepoint, OneDrive, or Google Drive can go a long way to quickly getting key information into employees' hands.
- **Instructional design (Id).** Just because it's intended to be short doesn't mean you should abandon key principles of instructional design. Identifying core needs, creating something that is engaging for people to learn from, and being intentional about how, when, and where it should be delivered are all essential considerations.
- **Games (Ga).** Introducing or refreshing people's memories using a gameshow- or trivia-inspired theme can make short bursts of information more engaging and interesting. Creating a series of microlearning pieces that align with a theme or story (like you can find in many board games or role-playing games) can offer a common thread to an extended series of short bursts of content.

While it's important to experiment with microlearning and see just how it could fit into your organization, here are a few final thoughts about how to freeze this element into place and make it a solid, lasting part of your overall learning strategy:

- **Develop or use microlearning when it meets a need.** There will always be trendy movements in learning and development that enjoy popularity and the spotlight—almost like the flavor of the month. I've seen this happen with the rise of microlearning as organizations push for their employees to spend less time "offline" in training and more time focused on their jobs. While there are many reasons to incorporate microlearning as part of an overall strategy, one of those reasons is not "Because everyone else seems to be doing it these days."

- **Begin with the end in mind.** Microlearning initiatives can be much more powerful when they're intentionally designed as part of an overall training program. You probably can't teach a complete, complex process or concept solely using short video clips and job aids. However, if you leave a complex process or concept to a one-off training experience, people may not always recall everything they need to do when they need to actually do it. Designing a robust plan before you begin to develop your learning program will lead to the best results.

Element 44
Goal Setting (Gs)

Any training program participant should have a solid answer for the question: What's in it for me? Creating an experience that is relevant and can help learners solve an immediate problem is a basic tenet of adult learning.

Often when I offer a webinar, I'll ask registrants to share something they hope to learn from the session. This is a very soft (informal) way to help with goal setting, which is an element that you can formally or informally incorporate into your training design. At its core, the element of goal setting is an attempt to ensure learners know exactly what's in the learning experience for themselves.

Setting SMART goals is a common place to begin. If you've not used SMART as a strategy for goal setting, these are the core properties:

- **Specific.** Any goal should be targeted to a particular area of knowledge, skill, or ability on which to focus.
- **Measurable.** Whether a qualitative (I'd like to perform with more confidence) or quantitative measure (I'd like to increase the number of sales that I close), there should be some language in a goal that allows you to see if there has been progress.
- **Action-oriented.** Some variations of the SMART model also use words such as *attainable* or *achievable*. I don't see enough variation in those properties to differentiate them from the "R" (realistic), so I prefer the "A" in SMART to be action-oriented. Action-oriented goals include the specific steps that a learner should take to turn their goal into reality.

- **Realistic.** Setting a goal that is impossible to achieve may be a noble dream, but it's a waste of time and effort. Ensuring participants set goals that can be reasonably achieved in the context of their skill level, position in the organization, and responsibilities will provide the best opportunity to put what they've learned into practice.
- **Time-bound.** Having a date by when the goal should be hit is an important way to hold learners accountable and ensure some degree of immediacy when it comes to applying new skills.

A common goal-setting strategy is to provide an action plan for participants to complete at the end of a training program. During longer training programs that cover many concepts, I like to distribute the action plan at the beginning of the session and make sure there is time during content transitions for participants to capture action plan ideas (instead of making them wait until the end and hoping they remember some of the earlier concepts that were covered).

If you're searching for ways to freeze this fluid concept, consider incorporating the following ideas as strategies into your future training design:

- **Provide a self-assessment.** Whether participants are looking forward to your course or they've been told they need to complete it by their supervisor, offering a self-assessment for them to identify areas of strength and areas for development can provide guidance and structure for where they should be setting their goals.
- **Send a pre-course goal-setting sheet in advance.** If you are in the advantageous position of having contact information for your participants in advance of a course, you can send a goal-setting form to help them calibrate expectations for the course and hone their attention to the areas they think will be most helpful. Encouraging participants to share the form with their supervisor can add a level of accountability and support.
- **Send post-course goal reminders.** Some course instructors ask participants to complete an action plan using two-ply NCR (No Carbon Required) paper wherein goals are written on the top ply and copied to the second ply. Participants hold on to the original and are sent the copy of their action plan 30-, 60-, or 90-days after the training program to remind them of their goals. Something similar can be done with e-learning content by generating an

automated email to remind people of the goals they set at the end of the course.

There are several elements you'll want to consider bonding to goal setting:

- **Supervisor support (Su).** No matter how self-motivated your participants are, ultimately it is their supervisor who can hold them accountable, encourage them to follow through on their goals, or (in the absence of goals) can encourage them to focus their attention elsewhere. For a training program to be effective, you'll want to find ways to avoid that last scenario. Identifying potential strategies by which you can help supervisors set goals with their direct reports as well as make them aware of the goals participants craft for themselves can make the difference between an interesting training program and an effective training program.

- **Follow up (Fu).** While action plans are an important element to many training programs, using a variety of follow-up strategies to remind participants of their goals and why your content was important can encourage transfer to the real world.

- **Instructional design (Id).** Like many other elements, goal setting cannot be a casual afterthought. Offering ways to help learners identify areas for improvement and giving them structure for goal setting throughout a training program can ensure goals are meaningful and more likely to receive follow through.

Reflection: Should Your Liquid Elements Remain Fluid, or Should You Freeze Them in Place?

Liquid elements allow for a lot of flexibility, although some may benefit your team or organization by being frozen in place and applied consistently. When you think of how you will use each of these elements, do you think they should remain fluid (liquid state), have some consistent elements while remaining flexible (slushie state), or always be used in a consistent and uniform manner (frozen state)?

Decide where each of these elements should fall when used within your organization, and in the appropriate column of Table 2-3, write some notes on what the element would look like when put into action. (For example, if you think supervisor support should be frozen, then write some notes in the frozen column for how you would freeze it in place, who needs to be involved, how it would be communicated, and how people would be held accountable.)

Table 2-3. Lab Counter or Lab Freezer?

	Liquid (Flexibility is needed any time this element is used. It will look different depending on the initiative.)	Slushie (This element will be adjusted on a case-by-case basis.)	Frozen (This element should be applied consistently. It should be codified into the organization's policies and procedures.)
Supervisor Support (Su)			
Measuring for Effectiveness (Me)			
Learning Boosts (Lb)			
Spaced Learning (Sl)			
Follow Up (Fu)			
Assessment (As)			
Mentorship (Mn)			
Coaching (Co)			
Microlearning (Mc)			
Goal Setting (Gs)			

Chapter 3
Radioactive Elements

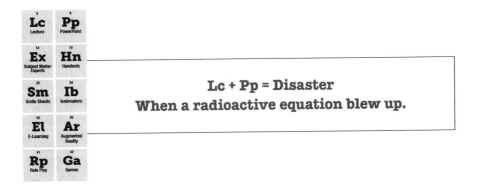

"Be careful what you wish for, you might just get it." Those words kept rolling around in my mind as I considered what I'd gotten myself into.

For two years, I'd been trying to convince our CEO and chief talent management officer that we needed to create a director of organizational learning position (and that I was the right person for the job). They finally agreed, and now I was worried that they were wondering what I was doing with all my time.

As our organization expanded, new people were being hired and needed to be onboarded in quick succession, but hiring managers refused to send their new employees to our onboarding sessions.

"Look," one senior manager said to me, "we're hiring people because we need to fill these roles right away. I need my people learning their job, I don't need them waiting to start their job so they can sit in a room and listen to people talk and show slides for three days."

Our onboarding program had become toxic, and I honestly couldn't counter their argument. Sequestering new employees in a room for three days and parading department representatives in front of them to deliver PowerPoint-based lectures really didn't seem to add much value. If I didn't figure something out, the whole brand of our new learning and development function was in danger of becoming radioactive, shunned by my colleagues, and with good reason.

What Are Radioactive Elements?

Radioactive elements are 11 of the most powerful yet most dangerous elements known to the L&D world. They are commonly used training tools, practices, and resources and can offer tremendous power when used in small doses. If used improperly (as is too often the case), they can be extremely combustible and contaminate the reputation of the element, the trainer, *and* even training itself. The radioactive elements are lecture (Lc), PowerPoint (Pp), subject matter experts (Ex), handouts (Hn), smile sheets (Sm), icebreakers (Ib), e-learning (El), augmented reality (Ar), role play (Rp), games (Ga), and data (Dt).

Lecture (Lc) and PowerPoint (Pp) have a well-deserved reputation for being overused and abused, clouding our best intentions and creating toxicity between us and the learners we're responsible for helping.

In his book *Brain Rules*, John Medina reminds anyone who lectures that emotions garner attention. Learners don't need, nor can they remember, every detail, and the brain cannot multitask. Not being able to cognitively multitask means that participants can't pay attention to your presentation if they're busy reading every word on your slide.

Lecture isn't inherently a bad element, but if it doesn't follow a format that allows the brain to absorb and process information it *becomes* inherently bad. The same applies to any of the radioactive elements. Many participants believe it's OK to come late to a training session that begins with an icebreaker because the opening activity holds little value. However, when icebreakers are judiciously and thoughtfully designed and delivered, they can help illuminate the entire presentation's purpose.

Even something as simple as putting together handouts requires thought. If you integrate your handout design with your instructional design, you can open a world of possibilities far beyond a boring, run-of-the-mill worksheet that your learners won't bother to take with them at the end of your session.

Let's take a look at each of these 11 elements in more detail.

Element 5
Lecture (Lc)

At its core, lecture can be defined as simply talking about content. In fact, lecture may be the single most prominent method of content delivery known to man. It can take many forms—from standard college classes and Sunday church sermons to TED Talks and storytelling. In its purest form, lecture is a broad concept whose primary properties feature:

- One-way presentation (speaker to audience)
- Verbal delivery of information

Lecture holds certain advantages over other content delivery methods. Learning architect James Goldsmith (2014) suggests that lecture is encouraged when:

- Subject matter experts (SMEs) need to discuss certain techniques or report on new knowledge in their field
- Time constraints mean that the delivery needs to be tightly controlled
- A speaker can demonstrate their passion about a topic (think TED Talk)
- Content is carefully scripted and needs to be delivered in a consistent, repeatable method (think videos or podcasts)
- There is so much facilitation in a lesson that there is a need for a different instructional strategy

Of course, if you subscribe to the idea that an instructor must be accountable to the audience, ensuring audience members are following along and enhancing their knowledge, skills, or abilities, then lecture can also present a challenge. Due to the one-way nature of this element, there is inherent difficulty in determining whether audience members are processing the information being delivered (or whether they're simply making eye contact while their mind wanders off to what they need to buy at the grocery store or who might win the big game this weekend).

For those most comfortable with the lecture format, several elements can bond with it to add instructor–learner accountability.

Some suggested bonds include:

- **Audience response (Re).** As you'll discover in chapter 4, "Solid Elements," audience polling can immediately engage your learners by asking them a simple question to which they can respond without feeling pressure or risk. This element can help empower them to add to or inform the way you tailor your session content through their responses.
- **PowerPoint (Pp).** Offering powerful visual aids or highlighting key points on a slide can enhance the learner experience. If you want more information on how this can be done, watch any presentation by Steve Jobs.

- **Quiz software (Qz).** Similar to audience polling, when you integrate quizzes or other options that force your audience to think about the topic, it suddenly becomes more relevant in the moment.

Keep in mind that while lecture is not inherently dangerous, it has earned its reputation as a radioactive element in large part because of its overuse. It may be easy to default to lecture as a means of content delivery, but there are a variety of other ways to deliver information and keep your audience engaged.

If you'd like to reduce your dependency on lecturing, you could substitute these delivery methods:

- **Conduct a gallery walk.** Place information and artifacts about key concepts on posters or at stations around the room. Break your learners into groups and have them rotate around the room and examine everything. Then, have them share their key findings or lead a round of Socratic questioning.
- **Show a video.** A video can feature a world-renowned expert, a speaker who is passionate about the topic, or animations that bring concepts to life. Regardless of how many times you show a video, it will always provide a consistent delivery.
- **Reveal a top 10 list.** Why plow straight through your content when you can break it up? Top 10 lists have been around for a long time (look up "David Letterman" for a great example). Or, if you're only presenting three key concepts, you can make it a top three list—"top 10" is just a way to categorize your content delivery strategy. Regardless of the number, a list that's clearly broken down by topics can help alleviate the monotony of what would otherwise be a continuous flow of information.
- **Read an article.** Similar to videos, distributing an article for your participants to read can provide access to consistent delivery of information, research, or world-renowned subject matter experts. Unlike lecture, articles allow learners to go at their own pace and visually identify key pieces of information.
- **Provide a case study.** Whether the case study is written or verbal, offering true-to-life examples of your content or concepts may help your learners relate to the information in a more concrete way.

Element 6
PowerPoint (Pp)

PowerPoint is the software tool that has had arguably the biggest impact on business meetings, professional development sessions, and classroom instruction since, well, ever. It was unleashed on the world in 1987 primarily as a tool to design and generate overhead transparencies. Even though overhead projectors are now considered obsolete relics of pre-Y2K technology, the basic PowerPoint interface has not changed much since it first came to market (just Google "PowerPoint interface 1987" if you'd like to see how little the look and feel of PowerPoint has changed between then and now!).

The variety of features packed within PowerPoint, however, has changed greatly. These features, when combined with good elements of instructional design (Id) and visual design (Vd), can be all that stands between an element that lights up your presentation and one that wreaks havoc on your learning environment for the duration of the experience.

Consider the core properties of PowerPoint:

- Computer-based visual design tool
- Ubiquitous in meetings and educational sessions around the world, regardless of culture, language, nationality, or computer system

If you search for how to use PowerPoint most effectively, you'll find a wide range of so-called expert advice:

- "No more than 20 words per slide."
- "Limit the use of bullet points."
- "Don't use bullet points."
- "Use powerful imagery."
- "Don't use clipart."
- "No more than three fonts."
- "No more than three colors."

The problem with this advice is that it's being given to you (mainly through internet searches) without any knowledge of your presentation.

If you're giving a TED Talk or introducing a new Apple product, then few or no words is the standard. If you're giving an executive briefing, then you're going to need some bullet points so that you can leave your document behind when the C-level group dismisses you before you're finished the presentation.

Be sure to think about your overall PowerPoint strategy. I like to think of PowerPoint as a sort of co-facilitator—it should never overpower me or my message, but it can be a very handy assistant.

While I have a lot of opinions on the appropriate use of PowerPoint, there are many people who have come before me who have written some very smart things about how to more effectively use this radioactive element. If you're looking for more information from some of these smart people, try:

- Anything written or said by Nancy Duarte (begin with her book *Slide:ology*)
- Jesse Desjardins' viral slideshare presentation (viewed almost 6 million times) entitled "You Suck at PowerPoint!"
- Melissa Marshall's four-minute 2012 TED Talk (viewed 2.5 million times) entitled "Talk Nerdy to Me"

Some suggested bonds for PowerPoint include:

- **Audience response (Re).** Many audience polling applications integrate with PowerPoint so that you can mix audience responses into the flow of your slide presentation. Depending on the application, you can inject multiple-choice polls, open-ended responses, or responses that build word clouds into your visual display.
- **Lecture (Lc).** While there are dangers in the PowerPoint/lecture combination, a tight, well-crafted lecture can provide key insights about the imagery contained in a slide deck.
- **Video (Vi).** Bringing appropriate video content into your session can offer an engaging departure from still imagery. The caution here is to ensure you follow copyright laws.
- **Screen capture (Sc).** The quality of the images you use in your slideshow matters, and screen capture software can make it easy to grab high-resolution images.
- **Visual design (Vd).** While PowerPoint has a lot of built-in tools to assist with your slide layout, having a basic understanding of visual design principles will help you put together more attractive and effective slides.
- **Games (Ga).** Just because you're using slides doesn't mean that every slide needs to have talking points. Using the full power of animations and triggers in PowerPoint, you can add audience interaction and engagement by creating *Jeopardy-* or *Family Feud*–like games.

To reduce your dependency on PowerPoint, try using:

- **Flipchart (Fc).** Once you advance a slide, it's gone. If you hang a flipchart on the wall, it will be with you for the duration of your presentation. A flipchart can come in several different forms, including pre-crafted pages you design prior to a session and then reveal when the moment is right, and dynamic pages you or your learners can build upon during discussions and brainstorming segments.
- **Handouts (Hn).** When I've been asked to re-imagine courses for clients, I've found one of the best ways to reduce the number of slides in existing PowerPoint presentations has been to move a lot of the detailed or technical content into a participant guide. Handouts or participant guides can be used as note pages or worksheets to enhance activities, and your learners can take these resources home and use them as job aids long after your presentation is over.

Element 14
Subject Matter Experts (Ex)

Subject matter experts (SMEs) are generally very smart, busy, and passionate about their area of specialty. These characteristics make them extremely valuable assets for you as you put together a training program, but they can also lead to frustration on everyone's part if you're not able to appropriately channel their energy.

There are several keys to harnessing the element of subject matter experts. The first is to find the best fit for your project. Several years ago, my organization, Endurance Learning, released a checklist to help learning designers prepare potential SMEs to provide expertise on a project (Figure 3-1). Although I've never seen a job description for the role of subject matter expert, they're prevalent in organizations around the world, with core properties such as:

- Significant experience, education, or expertise on a specific topic
- Few (if any) official job responsibilities that include "help other people put together a training program based on your expertise"

Once you've identified (or have been assigned) the SME with whom you'll work, there are several questions you'll want to ask yourself before you begin to spend time with them:

- **How will you ensure role clarity, establish a communication rhythm, and agree upon deadlines?** While SMEs are generally busy people, you will probably need to check in with them on more than

Figure 3-1. Subject Matter Expert Qualification Sheet

Quality	Yes or No	Clarifying Question	Notes
Deep content understanding	☐ Y ☐ N	Is this person a jack of all trades or a master of one? SMEs should be a master of their domain.	
Unique experience and/or perspective	☐ Y ☐ N	Does this person have an experience with the subject that is unlike others familiar with the content?	
Demonstrated willingness to share	☐ Y ☐ N	SMEs spend a lot of time learning everything about their subject. A good SME has a history of sharing their information by writing help documents or coaching others.	
Available	☐ Y ☐ N	SMEs tend to be busy, especially if training is related to a release or initiative. Is this person available during all review periods even if the timelines are extended?	
Training ambassador	☐ Y ☐ N	Does this person believe in the training that is being delivered?	
Cross-domain understanding	☐ Y ☐ N	Do they simply know how something works or do they truly understand how the information interacts with other information?	
Project-specific quality	☐ Y ☐ N	Does this person have experience with this particular training project so they can incorporate case studies, stories, or real-life anecdotes?	

one occasion. The way in which you do that, as well as the frequency with which you'll need to connect, should be clear expectations that are agreed upon from the start. These are basic yet crucial questions for managing any successful training project.

- **What problem is the training program looking to solve?** This will help ensure laser-like focus for your work. You should share your learning objectives with the SME to be sure you haven't missed any key learning points that will help your program address the problem that needs to be solved.

- **What information will you need from the subject matter expert?** Will you be OK if your SME just dumps a bunch of files on you and tells you they've done their job? Or will you need their help going through the information? Answering these questions will help ensure you keep the amount of information you need to process to a minimum and your SME won't waste time searching for or giving you access to superfluous information.

- **If you need the subject matter expert to create content, case studies, or other materials, how will you work with them to make sure you get exactly what you need?** Being respectful of their time; the more structure you can offer for the information you need and how you need it will help everyone involved. Exercise patience and understanding, knowing that your SME will generally not bring a thorough understanding of adult learning to the table. Even after you've provided structure and clear guidance on what you need, chances are good that you'll need to synthesize, refine, reformat, and restructure the information being shared with you before you can call a training program final.

- **If you would like the subject matter expert to present to your learners, how will you help ensure a positive experience for all involved?** Help prepare your SME by reviewing their talking points and slides to make sure any presentation is tight (and eliminating nice-to-know-yet-superfluous-to-the-learning-objectives information). Preparing your learners with questions they should be thinking about can help focus their attention prior to turning things over to the SME.

Once you've determined how you'll work with your SME, there are several elements that can form a strong bond:

- **Dialogue education (De).** Dialogue education is an element that can make the difference between a boring lecture and an effective, engaging presentation. Helping a subject matter expert identify the importance of principles such as immediacy (how will the information help solve a problem tomorrow?); ideas, feelings, and action (how can you connect concepts, emotions, and actions?); and engagement of the learners (how do you get learners to be active participants in their learning?) can lead to a positive experience for both presenter and learner.

- **Lesson plan (Lp).** Keeping in mind that your subject matter expert won't know much about dialogue education or instructional design, it will probably be up to you to develop a lesson plan for your SME to follow.
- **Instructional design (Id).** Integrating key instructional design steps that help to activate learners' prior knowledge, and giving them an opportunity to discuss or experiment with your subject matter expert's content, can make the difference between interesting information and a presentation that learners will remember and act upon.
- **Email (Em).** Not everything will be covered or answered during one training program. If your subject matter expert is willing to share contact information, the interactive element of email can be an important tool to allow learning, curiosity, and questions to flow after the program has finished.

A subject matter expert may not always be available or may not always be the most appropriate person to present to your learners. If that is the case, you could instead:

- **Show a video.** Subject matter experts generally make money for your company by doing things other than presenting in front of groups. Capturing a SME on film allows you to control their message in a tightly packaged video and frees them from the burden of repeatedly needing to appear in front of a training class.
- **Share an article or case study.** There may be times when you'd like to bring the voice of some of the smartest people in the world into your training program, but unfortunately you don't have them on speed dial. Finding an article (that you have permission to distribute) or a case study on the topic can bring an outside, expert voice into your training program without the hassle of turning over your lavalier.
- **Take the mic.** As long as you have some degree of mastery with the content, you don't necessarily need a subject matter expert to present. Combining good instructional design, facilitation skills, and subject matter knowledge can provide your learners with a sound foundation. However, one note of caution—make sure you don't rely on your

facilitation skills to overcompensate for a lack of knowledge about a topic. According to research published in *Training Industry* magazine, "If trainers don't master the content they are delivering, that weakness could overshadow their delivery skills" (El Kholy 2017).

Element 15
Handouts (Hn)

Handouts, participant guides, user manuals, and job aids can serve as reference materials and can keep the learning lights on for participants for days, weeks, and even years after a training course. They can also turn them off if the handouts are not designed with intention and purpose.

There is one key property that characterizes element 15: hard copy collateral provided to learners.

As with all parts of your training program, if you want to get your handouts right, you should be thinking about any collateral you plan to distribute as part of the overall instructional design process. For example, you could simply provide a self-assessment for your learners to complete as they begin your course that looks something like Figure 3-2.

Figure 3-2. A Sample Learner Self-Assessment

Question	Yes	No
Are you comfortable discussing new services with your customers?	☐	☐
Do you currently ask your customers or prospects questions to learn about their needs?	☐	☐
Do you currently consider yourself a salesperson?	☐	☐
Are you currently able to answer every question posed by your customers or prospects?	☐	☐
If you lose a sale and nobody is around to hear it, did you lose a sale?	☐	☐
Do you sell products?	☐	☐
Do you sell services?	☐	☐
Do your customers like talking about their business?	☐	☐
Do you sell solutions?	☐	☐
Are you comfortable using consultative selling techniques?	☐	☐
Do you know enough about our services to offer them to your customers?	☐	☐

Or, you could offer them a handout, which has much more potential to engage them and create a sense of curiosity for the remainder of the program.

In this program we were asked to design a training session for a *service* and deliver it to a group of employees who had only ever sold *products*. That they were now being asked (or better said, *told*) to learn about and sell services had become a very touchy subject. To pique our learners' curiosity and add a little controversy, we put the idea of selling this service on trial. When learners entered the room, they would not simply find a conventional checklist at their seats, but rather they would find a copy of Figure 3-3.

Figure 3-3. A More Engaging Sample Learner Assessment

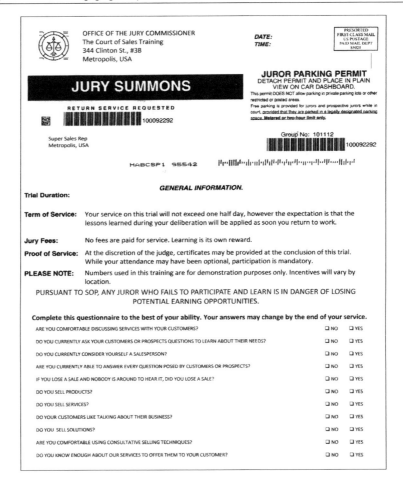

As you can see, it's still a questionnaire and it has the same questions as Figure 3-2, but it offers a very different feeling for the entire learning experience.

Other common handouts thrust upon learners are PowerPoint slides. However, it's important to keep in mind that slides and handouts serve two very different purposes. Working with one client, we were able to remove approximately 300 (!!!) slides from a two-day presentation deck by moving much of the information into a printed participant guide. This allowed the slides to be used specifically for visual cues to guide the presentation.

If you're planning to distribute your slides as handouts, you may want to make some edits before you hit that print button. (If they can get all the information from your printed slides, learners may be less inclined to listen to all of your brilliance.)

One quick, simple way to modify your slides before converting them into handouts is to remove key information. Then, your learners will have to invest some energy into listening for key concepts. For example, instead of providing a complete set of information on each slide (see the slide on the left in Figure 3-4), you can modify it to create a fill-in-the-blank activity (the slide on the right). This should increase learner engagement (and hopefully retention).

Figure 3-4. A Complete Slide Versus What Goes in the Handout

Compelling Visual Aids	Compelling Visual Aids
• Eliminate clip art	• Eliminate ____ ____
• If you're going to use an image, pay for it (we shouldn't see watermarks)	• If you're going to use an image, ____ ____ ____ (we shouldn't see watermarks)
• Stay consistent with fonts and colors	• Stay ____ with fonts and colors
• Sketch it out, first	• ____ ____ out, first

You don't need a degree in graphic design to create effective handouts, but bonding your materials with the following elements can help:

- **Visual design (Vd).** Incorporating the element of effective visual design is essential to having handouts that are professional looking, engaging, and memorable—something your learners will want to hold on to. It also demonstrates respect for your learners by not giving them something that looks like it was thrown together minutes before your session was about to begin.
- **Learning objectives taxonomy (Lo).** As with all aspects of your training program, your handouts should align and help accomplish

your learning objectives. The more tangential your handouts, the less likely your learners will find them useful and take them at the end of your program.

- **Instructional design (Id).** As you can see from the jury summons example, your handouts are an opportunity to further the narrative and arc of the instructional design strategy you've crafted for your program.

Element 23
Smile Sheets (Sm)

Smile sheets are the not-so-affectionate nickname given to Level 1 post-training evaluation surveys. They earned this nickname when someone decided to replace the numbers in a Likert scale–style evaluation form with a set of faces to choose from.

The content of this training met my expectations.	

You may be more accustomed to the traditional appearance of a smile sheet:

The content of this training met my expectations.	Strongly Agree	Agree	Neither Agree nor Disagree	Disagree	Strongly Disagree
	5	4	3	2	1

While smile sheets come in all shapes and sizes, with different questions and ways of attempting to measure the success of a training program, they have two core properties:

- Distributed following the conclusion of a training session
- Provide multiple-choice responses to gauge learner reaction

As discussed in chapter 2, smile sheets and Level 1 evaluation are designed to measure learner reaction and can be a helpful data point in how you evaluate the effectiveness of a training program. Radioactive element Sm becomes particularly dangerous, however, when it's used in large doses, or worse, when it's the only dose of evaluation administered to measure training success.

What are some reasons you might want to use smile sheets?

- While high scores don't necessarily mean learning happened, low scores can provide a red flag that merits further investigation.
- Open-ended, qualitative questions allow learners to share their insights and reactions to the session about which you may never have thought to ask.
- As long as you can craft good questions (and this is a tricky skill to master), you can gauge the learner's level of confidence in applying new knowledge or skills, which may be a predictor of success.

In his book *Performance-Focused Smile Sheets: A Radical Rethinking of a Dangerous Art Form*, Will Thalheimer (2016) writes that "the bottom line for me is that we need to get good feedback so that we can improve what we're doing." (Read this book, it will change the way you think about and create smile sheets!)

Because this element is more stable when it's bonded to other elements, you may want to consider adding one or more of the following to your evaluation formula:

- **Measuring for effectiveness (Me).** While smile sheets are an attempt to measure reaction and can offer one aspect of training measurement, measuring for effectiveness is going to make your Level 1 data more meaningful.
- **Follow up (Fu).** The enthusiasm that a learner may have for your content, as reflected in their smile sheets, may be genuine when they've been sequestered in a training room. When the daily routine of meetings, emails, phone calls, and office politics return, however, learner enthusiasm will naturally wane. Following up in the weeks (or even months) after a program has been completed can help remind learners why they gave your session 4s and 5s.
- **Assessment (As).** Remember how I mentioned that low smile sheet scores may indicate learning *didn't* happen, but high scores don't necessarily guarantee learning *did* happen? Integrating assessments into your training (through activities or written tests) can help identify where learning actually is and is not happening.
- **Levels of evaluation (Le).** This is a no-brainer. Considering smile sheets are Level 1 evaluation, it's important to keep in mind the role of other levels of evaluation in giving a more complete picture to any conclusions you'd like to make based upon the use of smile sheets.

While I have suggested potential substitutes for most of the elements in this chapter, I would like to write a few words about what *not* to use as a substitute for the smile sheet:

- **Butts-in-seats.** Also known as Level 0 evaluation, the butts-in-seats metric simply tells you how many people attended (or if you're online, accessed) a course. A low number here could tell you that your course is not well marketed or perhaps it's not relevant, but a high number is little more than a vanity metric. You may have had 15 or 150 or 1,500 attend your session, but that does not indicate whether those people got any value.

- **Net promoter score (NPS).** Originally developed as a marketing metric (How likely would you be to recommend our product to others?), the NPS has found its way into some training metrics. I confess that I once attended a webinar in which the presenter made a compelling case that a high training NPS could correlate to a learner's desire to apply new knowledge or skills, but unless you're very good with advanced analytics and are confident in your ability to separate correlation from causation, I'd stay away from using this to gauge the success of a training initiative.

Element 24
Icebreakers (Ib)

I've long subscribed to the idea that people don't want icebreakers, they want meaningful interactions. In fact, I've known people to skip the first 30 minutes of a meeting that listed an icebreaker as the first thing on an agenda because they had no desire to share their favorite food that begins with the same letter as the first letter in their name. So when a colleague in India suggested that we have a bunch of eye surgeons and high-powered board members pass a tennis ball around to each other to kick off a major international business meeting, I gave him the stink eye. When I lost the argument and my boss told me that we should do the tennis ball passing activity, I gave him the stink eye too. When we ran the activity and I observed that the room was abuzz with engagement and excitement to begin the meeting, I had to find a mirror so I could give myself the stink eye for being such an icebreaker snob.

This opening activity didn't work simply because it was a fun way to begin the day. It worked because there was a component of competition involved (in small groups, how quickly can you pass a tennis ball from one person to the next, with only one person allowed to touch the ball at any given point) and the participants (surgeons and successful business leaders) were highly competitive people. It worked because the CEO kicked off the meeting immediately after the activity by connecting the icebreaker to the meeting's theme of innovation. It worked because it was a high-energy introduction activity with a purpose.

While the mere mention of icebreakers can make learners want to run for the door, this is an element that can mean many things to many people, and has some appealing core properties:

- Allow learners to get to know one another
- Remove tension or discomfort around being in a new environment or learning a new topic

An additional property for icebreakers in a virtual environment (such as for webinars or virtual instructor-led training) is that they introduce people to the technology that will be used during the session (such as the chat feature, polling feature, or on-screen drawing tools).

Whether you're leading an in-person or a virtual session, using a well-designed icebreaker to ensure your learners are warmed up and ready to engage with your content and instructional style can be an immensely powerful opening element.

You can find instructions for a gazillion icebreaking activities if you run an internet search, but here are some common icebreakers:

- **Two Truths and a Lie.** Each person introduces themselves and shares two things that are true about themselves and one thing that is not, and the rest of the learners guess which is the lie.
- **Would You Rather...?** The presenter asks a series of binary questions such as "Would you rather have a superpower that allowed you to never have to sleep, or one that allowed you to pause time?" and then participants share their preferences.
- **Attendee BINGO.** All learners are given a BINGO card with descriptive statements (such as "Has a birthday in November" or "Has gone sky diving"), which they fill out by finding other learners around the room who fit those descriptions.

The key to your icebreaker being a valuable opening activity as opposed to a meaningless time-filler that risks tainting the rest of your session is the way in which you choose to debrief this element. Here are some debrief questions that you can customize to meet the specific needs of your icebreaker:

- We just asked you to answer a series of "Would you rather . . . ?" questions, but what does that have to do with today's topic? (This is a broad question and some responses from your learners may really surprise you.)
- How can the most recent activity serve as a metaphor for the work we have ahead of us?
- To be successful in this activity, you had to carefully listen to each person as they shared their truths and lies (or whatever you chose to have your learners share). What role does careful listening play when it comes to sales (or coaching or giving feedback or customer service or whatever your topic may be)?

Here are some suggested bonds for icebreakers:

- **Audience response (Re).** Especially when you are working with larger audiences or classroom-style seating—where it becomes harder to break the ice through more traditional means—incorporating technology and audience response polling can be a quick way to introduce a topic and get energy flowing in the room. For virtual presentations, the polling feature would be equivalent to a classroom-based software tool like PollEverywhere.
- **Quiz software (Qz).** Similar to audience response applications, integrating quiz technology such as Kahoot can help you survey what your audience knows about a topic, introduce friendly competition, and generate some energy.
- **Flipchart (Fc).** Having your learners record key information about themselves on a flipchart during the icebreaker and then posting that page around the room allows the information to remain visible for the duration of your session. If you've asked your learners to capture information about them that also relates to your topic, you can also refer back to what they've written throughout the session.
- **Games (Ga).** A quick game such as those mentioned earlier—passing the tennis ball or BINGO—can help boost the energy and warm up your learners. Take care to make sure there is a proper debrief to connect any game you play to the session topic.

- **Goal setting (Gs).** Some icebreakers can be as simple as "Tell everyone your name, where you're from, and one thing you'd like to be able to do now or differently or better as a result of today's session."

Due to the toxic reputation of icebreaking activities, the following suggestions can be substituted:

- **Tell a story or lead a guided visualization.** If you find yourself short on time or working with a particularly large audience or a room set-up that doesn't lend itself well to group interactions, finding a way to draw your learners into your topic may need to be a one-way street (presenter-to-learners). While this substitute does not generally allow learners to get to know one another, telling a captivating story or asking them to close their eyes and imagine something about your content can get their minds going and warm them to your topic.

- **Begin with an anchor activity.** Anchor activities are close cousins to icebreaking activities. While not necessarily designed to get learners to know one another, anchor activities are designed to help activate prior knowledge about a topic. Asking participants to think of their best (or worst) experience with the topic, having them offer a show of hands if they've ever been in a certain situation, or simply having them answer some flipchart questions posted around the room as they enter your training space are ways to activate prior knowledge without veering into the dreaded element of get-to-know-you icebreakers.

Element 32
E-Learning (El)

My first exposure to e-learning came in the early 2000s. I was working at a youth center and our program had just signed a contract with a company to provide e-learning content to my GED class. The students thought it was interesting and the content seemed pretty good. And it cost a lot of money.

Fast forward several decades and the cost of e-learning development has plummeted with the rise of rapid development tools such as Articulate Storyline and Adobe Captivate. In addition, many learning management systems (LMSs) allow administrators to publish content and videos, all in the name of e-learning. While it has become extremely affordable to produce, it doesn't mean every e-learning program is a high-quality learning experience.

Let's identify some key properties of e-learning content:

- Content accessed digitally
- Can be synchronous (in real-time) or asynchronous (accessible on-demand)

With these core properties in mind, e-learning content can take many forms—from a 10-minute, asynchronous module that you click through to answer questions to webinars or virtual instructor-led training to online college courses (and many things in between).

E-learning can be such a powerful learning tool because it can be delivered relatively inexpensively to many people across any geographic region. Unlike classroom training, which relies on the consistency of the presenter, e-learning content can be consistent every time. Organizations have also come to like e-learning because no travel budget is needed to deploy new content.

However, e-learning can also be an extremely toxic element that many employees don't want to touch, even if they were given hazmat suits. If a webinar isn't designed to be engaging, it's little more than an opportunity for learners to catch up on their emails on one monitor while you talk at them on their other monitor. When people choose to simply upload their PowerPoint deck to an LMS, which then converts the deck into "e-learning," it's little more than an invitation for learners to repeatedly click the next button to show they've completed the course.

To insulate your e-learning design against harmful gamma rays that can turn your learners into the Incredible Hulk, ready to smash their keyboards in anger and frustration, you may wish to bond your e-learning initiative with one or more of the following elements:

- **Measuring for effectiveness (Me).** There are many compliance-focused e-learning courses littering LMSs at organizations around the world. Whether you're generating a compliance course for a highly regulated industry or a module to build new knowledge or skills, measuring for effectiveness can help determine whether your investment in e-learning development was worth the effort.
- **Adult learning (Al).** Integrating principles of adult learning—finding ways to activate prior knowledge, ensuring relevant content, and addressing an immediate learner problem—can help prevent multitasking during webinars and mindless clicking through standalone e-learning modules.

- **Gamification (Gm).** Using elements of gamification—such as weaving a narrative throughout your module, integrating interactions with subtle feedback systems (perhaps a score goes up or down based on decisions the learner makes), or unlocking new content only when learners achieve certain objectives, can bring learning to life and provide incentive for learners to want to come back to your LMS.
- **Screen capture (Sc).** Have you ever been scrolling through an e-learning module or sitting through a PowerPoint presentation when you've come across a low-resolution or grainy photo? Screen capture tools like Snagit are inexpensive and help ensure your visual imagery is crisp and clear.
- **Visual design (Vd).** Adhering to standard principles of good visual design can make a huge difference between a conventional snooze-fest of a learning experience and something that engages participants at first sight. Making decisions about consistent placement of navigation buttons, cartoon versus photo imagery, and the amount of text (including font size and placement on the screen) are all important considerations.
- **Instructional design (Id).** Sometimes all someone needs is access to information in a place they can find it, when they need it. But if your goal is to help someone learn something, then simply uploading slides, resources, or documents to an LMS or lecturing at them in a webinar doesn't make it e-learning. Bringing in sound principles of instructional design to ensure learner needs are being met, activating prior knowledge, and giving your learners an opportunity to explore and practice using your content are all key elements that put the *learning* into *e-learning*.
- **Games (Ga).** Bringing in short games that challenge learners to use the information you've presented can offer an engaging and entertaining way to reinforce key elements of your module.

As with some of the other radioactive elements, you may not be able to replace e-learning content because your organization is looking to scale a learning initiative to many people or across various locations. Knowing that you need to generate an e-learning program, you may wish to familiarize yourself with some of the pioneers in the field who have been able to transform e-learning from a novel, digital experience to a highly engaging learning experience that can capture attention, change behavior, and improve skill sets.

- Michael Allen, who developed the earliest rapid authoring tools for e-learning development, speaks regularly at conferences and offers high-quality e-learning samples on his website. He literally wrote the book on e-learning: *Michael Allen's Guide to e-Learning: Building Interactive, Fun, and Effective Learning Programs for Any Company.*
- Cathy Moore is constantly writing articles and blog posts about creating meaningful, engaging interactions through effective instructional design. She wrote the book *Map It: The Hands-On Guide to Strategic Training Design.*
- David Anderson is the creative mind behind Articulate's weekly e-learning challenges and has grown a cult following among e-learning developers.
- Tim Slade is one of the most prolific writers about and creators of engaging e-learning modules. He has generated multiple courses that are available through LinkedIn Learning, speaks regularly, evangelizes effective e-learning design at conferences, and is the author of *The eLearning Designer's Handbook: A Practical Guide to the eLearning Development Process for New eLearning Designers.*
- Cammy Bean is an extremely creative and experienced e-learning designer who wrote one of the most genuine and accessible books on the topic of instructional design and e-learning, *The Accidental Instructional Designer: Learning Design for the Digital Age.*

Element 33
Augmented Reality (Ar)

When I was working through my list of radioactive elements, I was initially considering an element called "shiny objects" that would have included all the new technologies people get excited about but aren't necessarily the most appropriate for learning. In the words of my father: "You don't need to bring an elephant into class to teach the color gray."

After discussing this with some colleagues, I was persuaded to focus on one specific technology—augmented reality—that could fall into the broader category of "shiny objects" (a lot of the pros and cons of adopting AR should be kept in mind when you think of adopting other technologies that emerge in the near future).

Augmented reality has these core properties:

- Allows you to look at live images through a device (such as a smartphone or tablet), which overlays (augments) additional images
- Allows for real-time interaction with things that aren't really there

If you're not familiar with augmented reality, some pop culture examples include Nintendo's *Pokémon Go* app or the Instagram or SnapChat filters that give people dog noses.

While AR can be a powerful learning tool that boosts engagement, adds fun, and provides an element of reality that you otherwise couldn't bring into a training program when used under the right conditions, you'll want to keep the following warnings in mind to avoid a major training meltdown:

- **You get what you pay for.** While there continue to be new tools that make AR development financially accessible to people without any coding knowledge, very few people will be able to create a slick, easy-to-use, visually beautiful *Pokémon Go*–level application using those tools.
- **Just because you can isn't a good enough reason to put it into action.** Related to the point above, new tools are making it very easy to put together an AR-based activity that can be integrated into your session. But just like with any other activity, ask yourself if you're using AR technology to enhance the learning experience or because it's cool. **Your learners will be on a continuum of tech-savviness.** If you're expecting learners to download an app onto their own devices to access an augmented reality experience, be prepared for some people to get it in a snap, some to encounter an error, and some to look at you sideways because they're not sure where or how to download apps. And this assumes that all of your learners would even be open (or legally allowed) to downloading things onto their own devices. To avoid this, you may want to provide participants with a device that has all necessary apps already loaded and ready to go.

With those warnings out of the way, let's look at several reasons you *would* want to bring augmented reality into the training room:

- **It can replace (boring) slides and (bulky) materials.** For example, I've worked with a tire manufacturer who spends time training learners on how to identify why a tire may have come out of service. In traditional training settings, this can be accomplished by either showing a series of PowerPoint slides and having learners examine what they see, or by examining actual scrap tires that are brought into the training environment. AR would allow learners to point their device at a point in the room to overlay images of damaged tires and determine the cause of damage.

- **It can serve as a just-in-time job aid.** A colleague of mine began an Airbnb-based business and needed her housecleaning crew to replace supplies and return furniture to its original place, every time. While traditional checklists could help with quality control, using an AR-based app to quickly scan a room to see what is missing or out of place has helped her reduce the time she spends on QA efforts.
- **It can offer on-demand orientation.** Several years ago, I stayed at a hotel that had developed an AR experience where you could stand in a certain spot in the lobby, point your phone at that spot, and get a photo taken with an AR-generated celebrity. This concept can be used around offices as well by creating markers where employees can aim their device and be welcomed by AR-generated video (perhaps even of the CEO or other high-profile leaders). This can work for orientation to different physical spaces around the office, identifying where the copy paper or extra pens are kept, or introducing key policies and procedures.

The following elements can be bonded with augmented reality to enhance a learner's experience:

- **Learning boosts (Lb).** Learning boosts enhance learner retention, so adding an element of cool technology could offer a fresh take on a strategy that keeps your content in front of your learners in the days, weeks, and months after they've completed your session.
- **Adult learning (Al).** Adult learners want their professional development experiences to be relevant. Falling in love with AR technology without deploying it in relevant ways that enhance the learning can be a turn-off to many learners.
- **Gamification (Gm).** By its nature, augmented reality brings to life an element of fantasy—providing an overlay of something that's not actually in your classroom. Adding other game-like elements to your AR experience, such as points, a narrative, content unlocking, a quest, or teamwork, can bring additional engagement into your program.
- **Learning objectives taxonomy (Lo).** Learning objectives exist to keep your program focused. Any activity that you integrate into your

program—whether high or low tech—should help your learners do something very specific.

While AR can be a powerful tool, sometimes it truly is a shiny object. If you reconsider the idea of using augmented reality, the following may be suitable substitutes:

- **The real thing.** If it's not too big of a hassle to bring in actual equipment or not too big of an ask to bring in a person who otherwise would appear using AR, then just bring in the equipment or person.
- **PowerPoint slides or handouts.** There may be situations in which you are limited on time for your participants to use their devices to explore something using AR. Offering visuals on a PowerPoint slide or in a handout or manual can give your learners a "good enough" glimpse at the content you've introduced.
- **Analog games.** AR-based scavenger hunts or other activities or games can be replaced by old-fashioned scavenger hunts with handwritten (or computer-printed) clues and board games that people play in table groups to simulate experiences or introduce content.

Element 41
Role Play (Rp)

If you want your learners to groan, tell them lunch is running 15 minutes late. If you want your learners to groan louder, tell them that your next activity will be a role play. These are properties of the element role play:

- Attempts to simulate real-life interactions
- Uses guidance but not entire scripts

Role play can be an extremely important element that allows learners to practice using words, skills, and body language in a practice environment without consequences before they need to use them in real life. I've heard some learners object to role play because they don't want to get up in front of a group and look foolish, which is a perfectly reasonable concern.

Years ago, when I was a Peace Corps volunteer, a farmer asked if I wanted to accompany him to his farm and help with the daily chores. I laughed and said, "I don't know that you'd want my help milking the cows. I tried it once, and it was a disaster." He replied, "There's always a first time." Several weeks later when I went to his farm and he let me help milk the cows, it was a much better experience for the cow and for me.

The same holds true for the element of role play. Although it may be uncomfortable for someone to try on new knowledge, skills, words, or abilities the first time around, there will always be a first time. This is why pilots practice their landings in a flight simulator, surgeons practice on cadavers, and coaches run drills and scrimmages before playing an opponent. Salespeople, managers, counselors, teachers, and a whole lot of other people can improve their real-life skills if they include an element of role play.

That said, there is a very real danger that role play will be perceived as (or actually be) a waste of time if it is misused (or abused). For example, it can go sideways if:

- A role play scenario lacks structure and leads to hokey drama or easily resolved conflicts
- Learners are volun-told to get in front of the room and go through a role-play scenario without having practiced or grown familiar with the new concepts
- There is little or no structure applied to post–role play feedback

I've applied several strategies successfully to ensure that a role-play activity supplies maximum power to a training program, including:

- **Provide structure for everyone involved.** Most role-play scenarios feature someone who is supposed to be practicing a skill (such as a salesperson or hiring manager) and someone who is just going about their daily business (such as a customer or a job candidate). I prefer to have scenario information scripted for each person involved in the role play (Figure 3-5), which ensures the scenario focuses on the right skills (and that the scenario doesn't just resolve itself too easily because participants grow tired of the interaction).
- **Provide structure for feedback.** In her book *Learning to Listen, Learning to Teach*, Jane Vella offers 12 principles that make up the concept of dialogue education. These were outlined in chapter 2, and many will be familiar to those who have spent time in the classroom (the need for relevant content, the need to feel safe to participate, and so forth). One concept that people always want to learn more about when I talk about these principles is "praxis," or practice combined with reflection. Role play, if done properly, is the embodiment of this principle, since the act of role play is the practice, while the act of debriefing is the reflection. Giving everyone involved in the

role-play exercise—participants and other observers—a checklist, rubric, or other structured evaluation form can ensure post–role play feedback is relevant (Figure 3-6). To add an element of fun while

Figure 3-5. Information for a Salesperson and a Customer

Customer: Scenario 1	Help Desk Agent: Scenario 1
Call the help desk to let them know you cannot access any websites. Let the help desk know that you've been traveling recently. Prior to your travel (and even during your travel) this was not a problem. But now that you're back in the office, you just can't access any websites. **Only if the help desk agent asks:** You may share that, now that you think of it, someone in one of the regional offices from which you were working remotely during your travels made a few changes to your settings so that you could access their Wi-Fi connection while you were on-site.	You receive a call from someone at your organization who is well-known across your IT department for calling the help desk at least once (usually more) per week, asking for help on issues ranging from where to find certain software whose icons don't appear on their desktop screen to how to connect Bluetooth speakers so they can listen to music while at work. When this call comes through, you quickly check the help desk ticket requests and realize that you haven't heard from this person for the past few weeks.

Figure 3-6. Rubric for a Role Play Exercise Debrief

IT Department Customer Service Checklist		
Step	**Present?**	**Comments and Observations**
Listen	☐	
Repeat	☐	
Clarify	☐	
Document	☐	
Other observations (body language, attitude, elimination of technical jargon and terminology, etc.):		

trying to motivate observers to find as many concepts from the session as possible, I've also used a modified BINGO card as a role play observation form (Figure 3-7).

Figure 3-7. Sample BINGO Card

Facilitates with poise and confidence	Allows participants opportunities to explore and engage with content	Makes content relevant for the audience
Body language and energy creates positive learning environment	**FREE**	Effective summary and wrap-up
Pacing of speech allows participants to follow along	Checks for understanding	Uses visual aids as a supplement, not a crutch

- **Review with video.** Some learners aren't inclined to receive feedback very well, especially when it is seen as critical. In the face of feedback intended to be "constructive," it's easy for a person to grow defensive: "Thanks, but I don't think I actually said 'uh' and 'um' as much as you said I did. And I certainly don't talk with my hands as much as you said I did." To combat such defensiveness, try incorporating video. Ask an observer to use a smartphone, tablet, or some other device to record the role-play scenario, and then before giving any feedback, ask all participants (those involved in the role play and those observing) to review the video and fill out a feedback form. Once the video has been reviewed, no one should be able to argue over what did or did not happen. This offers training participants the same insights professional athletes gain when reviewing the video following a game. They can see themselves in action (as uncomfortable as it may be) and identify for themselves what they have done well and what they can improve upon. Here are two bonds for role play:

- **Assessment (As).** Role play can be a radioactive element when learners don't think it will help them learn something. Having a structured feedback component can be one way to bond role play with assessment. In addition, some training programs require learners to pass a culminating activity to complete the course. Using a role-play scenario in which a trainer or supervisor is equipped with a checklist or rubric to assess when a learner is competent in a new skill can add a very real level of rigor.

- **Goal setting (Gs).** This can be done at the start of a training session, then learners can compare their role-play performance with the goals they have already set; or it can be done following a role-play scenario when learners have received feedback and thus have greater awareness of where they should focus their attention for further professional development.

Role play isn't for everyone or every situation, so if you're looking for substitutes, you may wish to try:

- **Watching a video.** There are times when you may simply wish to show your learners a certain behavior. Having a video that models perfect or flawed behavior and asking participants to evaluate the behavior they've observed using a checklist can provide a consistent experience every time.

- **Providing a checklist or job aid.** When time is short, especially during new employee orientation or compliance training, you may not have time to integrate an effective role-play element. Providing a checklist or job aid can offer structure and guidance about the expected behavior.

Why isn't discussion listed as a possible substitute for role play? Many learners have asked if they could engage in a discussion about a new concept or avoid a role-play activity by simply saying, "Well, in this type of situation, this is what I *would have* said." Unfortunately, engaging in a discussion about or talking to the things you *would have* said isn't the same as actually saying the words to someone in a simulated (or real) situation.

Element 42
Games (Ga)

Several years ago, I worked with some colleagues to try to develop our own game for a training program on nonprofit board development (*The Nonprofit Board Board Game!*). We bounced ideas around, discussed them as a team, reviewed some of the content with subject matter experts, and thought we were ready. Then we piloted it, and it was a disaster. When our team debriefed this experience, we realized that creating a *Board Board Game* was a fun concept, but given the time we had for the session we were asked to develop, the game was too complex and there were some more straightforward and effective ways to introduce the concepts to accomplish our objectives.

Games can be hazardous to your training program when they are integrated more in the name of fun than in learning. Just because you've added a game to your program does not mean that you've magically gamified it. Games and gamification are different, which is why they are two separate elements on this periodic table.

In her book *Reality Is Broken: Why Games Make Us Better and How They Can Change the World*, Jane McGonigal discusses the plethora of benefits that game play can bring to the world and identifies four core properties of games:

- They have a goal
- They have rules
- They have a feedback system
- Participation is voluntary

Think of a game as a *single activity* while gamification is a *process* that involves applying game elements to a learning experience. While you may incorporate several games into your training program, you have not "gamified" it unless you've woven game elements throughout the program.

Games can be extremely fun, engaging, and add friendly competition that some learners find motivating. A note of caution here because I've also worked with many learners who have said they are absolutely not motivated by competition. If you're considering integrating a game into an upcoming program, you may want to think through your intended learning outcomes and decide whether a competitive game (one winner, everyone else loses) or cooperative game (everyone works together to achieve a common goal) would be more appropriate (Table 3-1).

Table 3-1. Comparison of Competitive and Cooperative Games

Examples of Competitive Games	Examples of Cooperative Games
• Jeopardy • Trivial Pursuit • Ticket to Ride • The Game of Life • Guess Who • Cranium • Settlers of Catan • Clue • Angry Birds • Apples to Apples	• Pandemic • Harry Potter Hogwarts Battle: A Cooperative Deck Building Game • Forbidden Island • Jumanji • Flashpoint • Sherlock Holmes Consulting Detective • Code Names Duet • Robinson Crusoe: Adventures on the Cursed Island

In an environment such as sales, where competition is part of the job description, a well-designed competitive game can simulate the real-life environment in which learners are navigating on a daily basis. If your training program is focused on skills such as team building, problem solving, or leadership development, a cooperative game may be more appropriate. Be prepared for some learners to naturally be more concerned about the rules, fairness, and winning than they will be about learning. Whichever direction you choose—competitive or cooperative game—be sure your learners understand that the game is a learning device and in the grand scheme of things, winning your game doesn't really matter.

There are some very smart people (and companies) who make a lot of money putting together games with elements that seem to work together smoothly and easily. Make no mistake, it is very hard to put together a game that makes sense and works well. The games you can buy when you're walking through the toy section of Target or Walmart are games that have been drafted, tested, revised, and refined over the course of time. There are a variety of games on TV, in toy aisles, and online whose mechanics and basic rules of play may inspire you to think of putting together a game for your training program. Keep in mind that directions to a game can take some time to grasp the first time a learner is introduced to it, so if you're planning to take inspiration from an existing game, you may wish to use the children's version, which often carries simpler directions but will still get you where you need to go.

Unlike when you play games with family and friends, there are very few instances in a training environment in which a game would be a standalone activity. These elements can be bonded to games:

- **PowerPoint (Pp).** PowerPoint can be a useful element in several different ways. Games like *Family Feud* or *Jeopardy* can be created using the animation and trigger functions. For board-style games, using PowerPoint to remind people of the basic rules of gameplay can be quite helpful.
- **Quiz software (Qz).** Using online quiz game platforms like Kahoot can take the onus of game-making off you. Many of these tools track each player's score and give you an opportunity to pause between each question to discuss the answer in more detail.
- **Adult learning (Al).** Integrate sound principles of adult learning, especially the principle that adult learners want their professional development experiences to be relevant and help them solve immediate work-related problems. If your game idea doesn't meet these criteria, you may want to rethink whether it is appropriate for your session.
- **Follow up (Fu).** During multiday or multiweek sessions, games can be an engaging way to review and follow up material covered during previous sessions. During a multiweek session we created for a client, we welcomed participants back to the second week by having them play a *Trivial Pursuit*–inspired game, which our learners found to be much more engaging than simply running down a bulleted list of concepts we had covered during the first week.
- **Rapid authoring (Ra).** Rapid authoring tools have become a staple of e-learning development. Breaking up screen after screen of content with some advanced development using animations and triggers can add fun and engagement to online learning. Depending on your objectives, there are many video games that can offer inspiration.
- **Microlearning (Mc).** Microlearning can come in many forms, but bringing games into short educational bursts is one way to combine learning with a fun experience.
- **Learning objectives taxonomy (Lo).** This is perhaps the single most important element to bond with games to ensure you end up with a powerful learning experience that is completely safe for public consumption. Any game you choose to integrate into a learning

experience should align with what your learners should be able to do as a result of the program.

If you're thinking of using games, here are several final helpful hints:

- **Make sure your directions are clear.** There is nothing more frustrating than sitting down to play a game and then getting confused by the directions even before you've made your first move. Poor directions can lead to confusion and frustration, turning what you hoped to be a fun learning experience into a disaster.

- **Think of using the junior edition as inspiration.** *Junior Monopoly* or *Settlers of Catan Junior* (or other "junior" versions) adhere to most of the same game mechanics but are simplified versions. Having simpler directions and fewer game variables can help make sure you don't spend too much time trying to get your learners to understand your game. The quicker the learners understand the game, the quicker they can get to learning your key points through them.

- **Keep testing, keep refining.** As with any experiment, creating games that are effective, engaging, and accomplish your learning objectives will probably take (at least) several iterations. Be patient and have fun with it. Once you have a working prototype, ask a co-worker, friend, spouse, or child to help you test the directions, flow of the game, and any mechanics you think you need to tighten. Refine the game based upon your observations, test it again, and continue to refine until you think it's ready for prime time.

Element 43
Data (Dt)

Did you know that, according to an industry study, a whopping 44 percent of all statistics used during conference presentations were made up on the spot?

That statement actually isn't true, but it sounded real, didn't it? Data can be such a powerful element to both establish credibility and capture the attention of your learners, but it's so easy for the power of data to be manipulated. Bad or misleading data holds the potential to contaminate the credibility of your initiatives or even you personally. Data should be used, but with an abundance of caution.

Let's take a look at the core properties of element 43, data (Dt):

- A collection of information to be analyzed
- Can be qualitative or quantitative

Data is all around us, and in the learning environment it is up to us to discern which data is useful and which would be inappropriate to share. Perhaps you've seen (or even shared) a variation of Dale's Cone of Experience (Figure 3-8).

Figure 3-8. Edgar Dale's Cone of Experience

On average, people remember. . . .

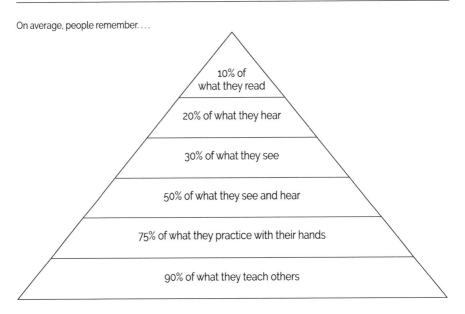

There are variations of this figure all over the internet attributed to educator Edgar Dale. There are quantitative numbers assigned to each category. It looks good and seems logical, right? It even aligns with the old proverb: Tell me and I forget, show me and I remember, involve me and I understand.

The problem with this graphic is that there is no *actual* data behind the numbers. Yes, Edgar Dale did publish a "Cone of Experience" in a textbook, but he never affixed numbers to his model. Recently, I read an article that used a variation of this model (with numbers attached). The article included a tiny author's note at the end in which the author admitted that while there was no actual data behind the numbers, he chose to keep the graphic (with the numbers) because he thought it would resonate with people.

Using made-up data in an effort to resonate with your learners is a terrible idea, and if they ever realize that you've led them astray, your professional credibility can vaporize instantly.

Several years ago I was at a conference when a speaker shared a statistic from a Microsoft study that was published in *Time* magazine. The entire audience was captivated when we learned that the human attention span had dropped from 12 seconds to eight seconds, and as a species our attention span was now shorter than a goldfish. This wasn't just a fun fact, it was a call to action! We had to create better e-learning content that was hyper-engaging so we could keep the attention of our learners.

The problem is, Microsoft never actually conducted or published any such study (there is, however, a real *Time* magazine article, which is a whole other conversation we should have at some point). The idea that the human attention span is shorter than that of a goldfish is a complete myth.

That we need to create better and more engaging e-learning content is no secret, but there's no need to use made up statistics, even if they seem like they'd resonate with learners.

Are you having some concerns about the data or statistics you've been sharing? Here are some ways to double check the veracity of your data:

- **Be skeptical of round numbers.** If you've ever done any research at all, how often have your numbers ended in a nice round 0 or 5? While it's not unheard of for a data point to end that way, it is rare (and many statistics also include decimal points).

- **Always check your sources.** Saying something like "a lot of surveys say" or "so many sources have concluded" leaves too much wiggle room and opens the door for urban legends to take off. Be sure any data you're planning to use is associated with a specific study or source. It also wouldn't hurt to verify the source or study being attributed as well. If you look at the Dale's Cone example, the data provided is often attributed to the National Training Laboratories. This is a real organization, but there is no research available that applies the data in the diagram to how people actually learn or remember.

- **Differentiate between data sources.** Some statistics come from scientific studies that have been rigorously vetted and published in peer-reviewed journals. Some statistics come through surveys that rely on self-reporting or respondents that are not representative of the general population. Not all data sources are equal, include the same margin of error, have undergone the same amount of rigorous peer review, or are neutral and unbiased.

To make sure that you're using the most powerful data available for your learning initiative, the following elements could help create useful bonds:

- **Audience response (Re).** Sometimes the most powerful data is the information generated by your own learners. Integrated live audience response tools that survey, poll, or ask open-ended questions of your learners can offer insights and data to which you can refer throughout your program.

- **Google (Gg).** Using Google to perform a quick double-check on the accuracy or veracity of your statistics can help prevent offering misinformation. Beyond the numbers, a Google search can lead you to articles and research that offers more context to the data you plan to share.

- **Change management (Cm).** Regardless of the instructional design model you choose, your initial step will be to analyze learner needs. Researching data that shows evidence for the need of your learning initiative, and then sharing that data with your learners, can be a powerful "what's in it for me" opening to your session.

If you can't find data to help bolster your content, here are a few substitution ideas:

- **Don't fret.** Not every concept requires scientific certainty. Don't lie about the strength of your content or try to manipulate your audience using deceiving statistics. Instead, be sure to apply logic and clear insights as to why your information is important, then allow participants to try your concepts out for themselves. Sometimes seeing (or doing) truly is believing.

- **Do question your content.** Every once in a while, it is important to question what we think we know. For many years I integrated a component revolving around learning styles into my train-the-trainer programs. Then I read an article that pointed out there was actually no research to support the idea that catering to a specific learning style had an impact on learning results. I did have to go through a mourning process in letting go of a belief I thought to be true, but then I dropped the learning style section and became a better, more evidence-based designer and presenter.

- **Use a model.** "All models are wrong; some models are useful" was a refrain that my professors preached over and over during my grad school years. The original "Cone of Experience" was a model. So are 70-20-10 and Kirkpatrick's Levels of Evaluation. There are many sales models and customer service models and coaching models and conflict resolution models. Similar to data, models have a story to tell; the question becomes what story are they trying to tell? Models can give a structure or framework that helps organize thoughts and they can be quite helpful as long as you understand their perspective. Real life can be messy and rarely fits into the neat boxes laid out through a model's framework.

Reflection: Handling Radioactive Elements With Care

Think about the ways in which you're currently using any of the radioactive elements discussed in this chapter. Place a mark on the Geiger Counter reader that corresponds to the frequency at which your training programs use the radioactive elements and decide if you need to consider alternative sources of energy in your initiatives.

Figure 3-9. Geiger Counter

Frequency of Use	Not Enough (-1)	Never (0)	Sometimes (+1)	Always (+2)	Ways I Can Improve the Use	Alternative Sources of Energy I Could Be Using
Lecture (Lc)						
PowerPoint (Pp)						
Subject Matter Experts (Ex)						
Handouts (Hn)						
Smile Sheets (Sm)						
Icebreakers (Ib)						
E-Learning (El)						
Augmented Reality (Ar)						

Figure 3-9 (cont.)

Frequency of Use	Not Enough (-1)	Never (0)	Sometimes (+1)	Always (+2)	Ways I Can Improve the Use	Alternative Sources of Energy I Could Be Using
Role Play (Rp)						
Games (Ga)						
Data (Dt)						

Chapter 4
Solid Elements

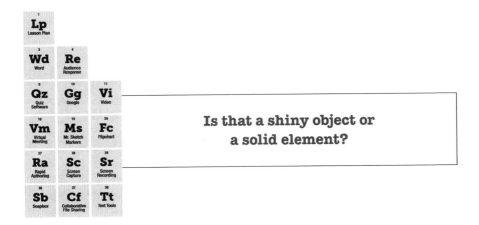

Is that a shiny object or
a solid element?

Several years ago, I sat in a meeting with a colleague who led training initiatives for our call center. She had a vision for a web-based tool that would allow call center staff to enter a keyword or two and have it pull up answers to frequently asked questions they might receive. "Does something like that exist, or could we build something like it?" she asked.

While her training was effective, there was a ton of information that the call center reps needed to be able to access at a moment's notice, and humans can only remember so much information. I thought for a moment. I was sure something like that could be built. It might cost some money and it would certainly take a little while to build, but it would be kind of cool to offer our staff a performance support tool that would put the right information at their fingertips when they needed it.

Then another idea popped into my head. "What if we had a written document—whether a Word document or a PDF—that simply had a clickable table of contents? If we could organize the table of contents so that call center reps could find the general category of information they needed at a glance, and then click on that category for more information, would that serve the same purpose?"

"I suppose it would," she said with a smile. "That seems like a rather simple solution. And I love it."

When it comes to learning and development, there is an insane number of tools—at all different price points from free to thousands (or millions) of dollars—in the marketplace designed and marketed to help us do our jobs better, more quickly, and more efficiently. Some of those tools are the right solution. Others hold lots of promise on the surface but are really just shiny objects that catch our attention and look sleek and inviting, but won't bring the results we need.

Of course, depending how it's used and the intent behind it, one person's shiny object could be another person's most important and solid tool. Sometimes it depends on what you need to accomplish and how you plan to use it.

What Are Solid Elements?

This chapter focuses on solid elements—training tools—and offers a variety of examples of ways that you can maximize them so they're more than attractive-yet-unnecessary toys that may yield disappointing results. First, let's take a closer look at what makes up a solid element.

The principal property that all solid elements have in common is that they are tools—whether tangible, physical tools or virtual, online tools—that trainers and instructional designers can use to create an engaging learning experience. Some, like Microsoft Word (Wd) and Google (Gg), are ubiquitous. Others have only recently gained traction. Tools such as audience response (Re) and quiz software (Qz) are a bit more viral in nature; they're not necessarily common, but when people see them in action for the first time, they quickly move to incorporate them into their own training sessions and presentations. This category also includes some newly discovered elements, such as Soapbox (Sb), which suggests that this periodic table is not an exhaustive list, and new elements of engaging learning design will continue to be discovered or created over time.

There are currently 15 solid elements: lesson plan (Lp), Word (Wd), audience response (Re), quiz software (Qz), Google (Gg), video (Vi), virtual meeting (Vm), Mr. Sketch Markers (Ms), flipchart (Fc), rapid authoring (Ra), screen capture (Sc), screen recording (Sr), Soapbox (Sb), collaborative file sharing (Cf), and text tools (Tt).

Unless talent development professionals are intentional about how to use a solid element, they cannot fully unlock its value. Similar to the way that cave dwellers applied logic and necessity to mold rock or metal into arrows for hunting and bowls for holding food, anyone wishing to make good use of these solid learning elements must apply intention so these tools can most effectively meet their needs.

For instance, using an online polling tool can be a cool visual aid, but is it necessary in a room with only seven participants? Equipping people with colorful, scented markers so they can write on flipcharts can keep learners awake, but what will you do with their flipchart notes once they finish an activity?

Few solid elements are intended to stand alone. For best results, you should mix them with liquid, gas-like, interactive, or even radioactive elements. What follows is a brief description of each solid element, along with some thoughts about how to bond them with other elements from the table to concoct a variety of engaging learning experiences.

Keep in mind that the Periodic Table of Amazing Learning Experiences highlights only 15 actual tools or categories of tools and is not intended to be an exhaustive list. If you're looking for a longer list of specific, individual tools trainers are using across industries, check out Jane Hart's Centre for Learning & Performance Technologies' annual list of the top 200 tools for learning.

Element 1
Lesson Plan (Lp)

The lesson plan leads off the list of 15 solid elements on this periodic table because it's a metaphorical beaker that trainers can use to mix many other elements.

I've gone back and forth with colleagues over the name of element 1. Some people use the term *presenter notes* or perhaps an even more formal variation of this element could be *facilitator guide*. For the purposes of this book, we'll stick with the term *lesson plan* and describe it with the following properties:

- Written narrative of a training session's sequence and flow
- Guidance on how much time to spend on any given topic, talking point, or activity

- Provides big-picture information that could include overall session goals, specific learning objectives, and materials to be used during the session

When asked to put together a presentation or training program, many people begin by opening up PowerPoint and generating slides that can include content and talking points, or perhaps they're given an existing deck and told to use it to create something new. I think beginning presentation design with a slide deck is a mistake, especially if you're looking to create an amazing learning experience for your participants. Organizing your thoughts using PowerPoint may mean that you're unconsciously turning over the power to structure your session to Microsoft software. PowerPoint slides have a very mechanistic, sequential order that is good for capturing talking points or displaying data, but not as effective when thinking through how to make sure people can do something new or differently or better as a result of your session.

When you begin by opening PowerPoint and jotting down your talking points, you may be limiting the way your learners could best absorb the information. Is it better for them to read through some bullets on a slide, or should they get out of their seats and visit stations that you've set up around the room as part of a gallery walk? Do you want to have information about your key points on a slide in front of the room for your participants to read, or do you want them to discuss what your key points mean to them and how they can use your content in their real lives by breaking into small groups?

When you create a lesson plan first, you may realize you don't even need slides for your presentation. A lesson plan allows you to think through the presentation's purpose, sequence, and flow without any restrictions or preconceived notions on how your content can be presented.

An internet search for lesson plans can yield many results; Figure 4-1 is an example of a lesson plan that I've been using (and adapting) for more than a decade. As you can see from this example, there are several key elements to a lesson plan.

Overall Goal

What is it that you or your organization want to accomplish? This is a big-picture goal that can set the tone and direction of the session.

Figure 4-1. Lesson Plan Example

Title of training segment:

Overall goal of training segment:

Date and time:

Learning objectives:

By the end of this training segment, the participants will be able to:

1.

2.

3.

Materials:

-
-
-

Procedures and instructional techniques:

Estimated Time	Content and Key Points	Instructional Technique

Learning Objectives

What should your learners be able to do by the end of the session? It's essential that this section uses participant-centered, action-oriented, observable language. This isn't what you want to accomplish or talk about, but rather what everyone in your audience will get out of the session.

Examples of this could include:

By the end of this session, my learners will be able to:

- Demonstrate the ability to navigate the five steps of our sales process.
- List the three steps involved in folding t-shirts for the floor display.
- Accurately enter data in our new Salesforce system.

Examples of learning objectives should never look like:

I plan to talk about how to identify and cultivate new sales relationships.

This speaker-centered statement may better fit into the overall goal of the session, but certainly doesn't qualify as an actual participant-centered learning objective. Examples of solid learning objectives would be statements such as:

- Participants will be able to use our sales model to engage a customer in a productive conversation.
- Participants will be able to enter customer data accurately into the new Salesforce system.

There are no "I" statements (such as "I will talk about" or "I want participants to know") because these are always learner-centered statements.

To create an effective learning objective, try this formula:

Timeframe + Name given to your audience + "will be able to" + Action-oriented, observable verb + knowledge or skill to be focused on

Here's how that breaks down:

- Timeframe (by the end of this module, by the end of this session, by the end of this month)
- Name given to your audience (participants, learners)
- "Will be able to"
- Action-oriented, observable verb (avoid verbs such as "know" or "understand" because it's very difficult to physically observe such actions as a facilitator. Instead, try using verbs that might answer the question, "How am I going to determine if they know or understand something?")
- The skills or knowledge they should gain (such as steps to a sales process or rationale for using a new computer system)

Materials

Listing materials that you'll use in a training session, such as markers, sticky notes, and voting dots, can help remind you what you'll need on the day of your session.

Procedures or Instructional Techniques

This is the section of a lesson plan in which you map out the specific sequence and flow of your talking points and activities.

- **Estimated time.** Assigning an estimated amount of time that you'll spend on each segment of your session will help keep the session running on schedule. Without this component, it's very easy to spend more time in certain areas earlier in your session, then have to rush through other topics or activities later in the session so you can still end on time. While you may not need to stick to your estimated time allocation if you see that participants could benefit by spending more (or less) time in a certain area, this part of a lesson plan will help you determine how much and where you may need to cut down on content or activities later on.

- **Content and key points.** You need not write out a verbatim script (in fact, I'd discourage you from doing so as the temptation to read off your lesson plan may be too great), but capturing key talking points and clear, specific activity instructions can help you determine how much time you need to spend in any given section of your session. I've often realized I need to allocate more time than I originally anticipated once I've spelled out the specific activity or discussion instructions in this section.

- **Instructional technique.** This is a section of the lesson plan in which you can simply describe how you plan to get your point across. Will you use lecture, tell a story, engage people in a small or large group discussion, use quiz software, or administer some sort of poll? Filling in this section will allow you to quickly determine if you have the variety of instructional techniques that you think would lead to an amazing learning experience. If you see "lecture" listed back-to-back-to-back-to-back throughout your lesson plan, you may want to think about breaking that up with discussion, gallery walk, or some other way to get the audience engaged. Alternatively, if you see that you're having participants change to a different activity every five or 10 minutes, they may eventually suffer from activity fatigue.

As with the other elements described in this book, these elements can be used as a standalone pieces for your learning program, but they often work best when bonded to one or more other elements from this periodic table. If you plan to use a lesson plan to develop amazing learning experiences, you may wish to bond it with one or more of the following elements:

- **Lecture (Lc).** Even when you're planning to use lecture as a central element of a training session, a lesson plan can help surround your content with other activities or instructional strategies to ensure your learners can do something new or differently or better. Using a lesson plan can help you identify *where* to fit in other activities beyond the lecture so you can determine whether or not your learners are "getting it."

- **Adult learning (Al).** Your learners want content that is relevant and can help them solve a problem. Using a lesson plan can help you completely map out a session that not only provides good content but also outlines activities you can use to make sure your learners see the relevance of that content and how it can help them solve a problem. A lesson plan can give you the space to plan out a few questions to ask your learners in advance of your lecture to help keep them focused. A lesson plan may also give you space to attach a post-lecture discussion to your training program so learners can solidify their understanding of how your content is relevant to them.

- **Subject matter experts (Ex).** There may be times in which you would like to (or have been instructed to) bring a SME into your session. Sharing a lesson plan with your subject matter expert can help focus their message and allow them to see how their presentation fits into the greater context of your session.

- **Virtual meeting (Vm).** The temptation to open PowerPoint and begin designing a virtual session is even greater than when delivering an in-person session, because virtual meetings rely so much more on PowerPoint to navigate the content and hold your learners' attention. Avoiding this temptation and beginning with a lesson plan for virtual sessions is essential to making sure you can use a variety of activities and features to provide an amazing (virtual) learning experience.

- **Soapbox (Sb).** As you'll discover in more depth when you examine element 36, Soapbox is a tool that can help you quickly concoct your own lesson plan. The lesson plan (or facilitator guide as the Soapbox software calls it) will allow you to determine how much time to spend on which activities. The added advantage of the Soapbox format is that it connects your learning objectives with activities designed to help accomplish those objectives.

As I'm sure you have deduced by now, a lesson plan is a tool specifically for instructor-led training, whether it's delivered in-person or virtually. While there isn't element for its e-learning equivalent, the storyboard, the general principle of mapping out your sequence and flow of content before you begin developing the learning experience will apply to e-learning as well.

Element 3
Word (Wd)

While there are other word processing tools (Google Docs certainly comes to mind), Microsoft Word is perhaps the most commonly used, having been released by Microsoft in 1983 and installed on any machine with Microsoft Office. It can be used to generate handouts, participant materials, facilitator notes, reports—some people even use it as a basic graphic design tool to lay out resources, job aids, and data.

While the uses vary wildly based upon need, the following properties will always hold true for Word:

- It's a word processing software
- Can be used individually or collaboratively

Just how does a plain old basic application like Word get a place on the periodic table of elements of *amazing learning experiences*? The answer is partly based on how you plan to use Word to create documents that are intended to supplement or enhance the learning experience. (The other part is a few paragraphs below, when you think of some elements that can be bonded to your use of Word.)

If Word documents are part of the formal learning experience, and if you want them to be used during and especially after your session, then the way you use some of the following features can make a big difference:

- **Font.** Is your font size large enough to be read by everyone who gets a copy of your document? (Word currently defaults to an 11-point font size, which is a common preference on documents from college papers to resumes; if you decide to shrink the font size to squeeze everything into a one-page document, recognize that some people may struggle to read your content.) What does your font choice say about the tone you wish to set? (Comic Sans sends a very different message than Calibri.) If you're cutting and pasting from other documents, is the font consistent or have you brought a mish-mash of fonts into one document?

- **Styles and headers.** Breaking up the information in your document can make it easier to read and process. When you use headings (from the style section of your menu bar), you not only break up the formatting of your document, but can also easily generate a table of contents for longer documents. Speaking of multipage documents, don't forget page numbers for easier reference.
- **Imagery.** Formatting your text isn't the only way to break up a document. Using photos, diagrams, or other drawings can literally illustrate the points you're trying to make. Keep in mind that Word was never intended to be a graphic design tool, so placing images in the exact location on the page that you'd like can be tricky.
- **Final printing.** How many copies will you need to make? Would you like to reduce the number of pages you're using by printing on both sides, or is there a reason that one-sided printing would be better? Would it be helpful to print different documents on different colored paper (so you could say something like , "Now if you'll turn to the yellow handout, you'll see…")? Will it be necessary (or just a nice touch) to print in full color rather than black and white? (Sometimes certain images, graphs, charts, or diagrams are much easier to read when printed in full color.)
- **Final document format.** If you're not planning to distribute your file digitally, then saving it as a Word document (or whatever format is convenient for you) is just fine. If you plan to distribute it electronically however, either via email or as a downloadable file in an e-learning module, you may wish to publish your file as a PDF. Saving as a PDF will lock in your fonts, styles, headers, and imagery location on each page so nothing weird happens when participants open the file.

Word can be an even more solid tool when it's bonded with any of the following elements:

- **Handouts (Hn).** It may sound obvious, but there are times you may refer to a document without actually bringing it into the training environment to distribute. If there's a document that learners should refer to or be able to access, you may want to consider making it a handout in your session.

- **Visual design (Vd).** Word may not be a graphic design tool, but that doesn't mean you can ignore how your document is laid out. If your document is easier to read, it becomes more inviting to use.
- **Virtual meeting (Vm).** Just because you're not with your participants in person doesn't mean you can't distribute handouts. In fact, when you upload documents that learners can download and print, virtual meetings feel a little less remote.
- **Collaborative file sharing (Cf).** Keeping your documents in your computer's local drive means that you're the only person who can access them. If your documents are meant for others to learn from, uploading them to your intranet, SharePoint site, or other organizational document repository can give your colleagues or participants access to information in their moment of need.
- **Instructional design (Id).** Keep in mind that the design of your Word documents can be a key part of your learning experience—not just by making it easier to read, but also keeping it thematic to your content. You can see some examples of what this means in chapter 3's section about handouts.
- **Website (Wb).** While collaborative file sharing is a good spot for internal documents, if you're working with external audiences, posting your Word documents and handouts to a course website or your homepage can make them readily available to others.
- **Email (Em).** Sending the Word documents and materials to participants following the session is a good way to keep your information front of mind and increase the likelihood they'll use your information, processes, or job aids.

Element 4
Audience Response (Re)

Picture yourself in a training session that you've been asked to attend by your supervisor, who is concerned about the recent quality of candidates and new hires at your organization. After an initial welcome, the speaker *insists* that you pull out your phone because she wants you to use it at various points during the session. Three minutes later, a slide like Figure 4-2 comes up, and you are asked to send a text message with your vote. The facilitator tells you to vote carefully because your answers will affect how she chooses to allocate time during the session.

Figure 4-2. Example of an Audience Poll

Which of the following would be most important for you to master today?
A. Creating better job descriptions
B. Developing effective interview questions
C. Generating a hiring matrix to compare interview candidates
D. Practicing behavior-based interview techniques
E. None of the above

Up until relatively recently, conference keynote speakers or professors could dazzle their audiences through interactive polls similar to Figure 4-2 by providing remote clickers that connected to the presentation. This offered a unique, real-time, interactive experience but could be expensive. (Not to mention the logistical pain of having to track down and collect the clickers at the end of the presentation!)

Audience interactivity has come a long way, and technology has created some new ways for presenters to engage participants through real-time polling that appears on the projector screen. Audience response software, also referred to as polling software, can be a quick and easy way to survey your learners and find out what they know, what they want to know, or what they're thinking about your content and presentation. Some of today's more popular tools include PollEverywhere, Mentimeter, and slido.

These are common properties in any audience response tool:
- Web-based software
- Audience can respond through text messaging or a website
- No additional equipment or hardware is needed as long as participants have a device such as a smartphone, tablet, or computer

Depending on the platform you use, you could engage your audience through multiple-choice polling, open-ended questions, or word clouds generated with participant responses. Some platforms also allow you to get into quizzing and games (which we'll cover with element 9, quiz software).

While more analog versions, such as surveying your audience by asking for a show of hands, can give you a general feeling for where people stand, audience response software allows you (and your audience) to see in real time the exact breakdown of the responses to your questions.

Audience response software can serve as a stand-alone element, but for best results you may wish to bond it with one or more of the following:

- **PowerPoint (Pp).** Most audience response software is able to integrate online polling with your PowerPoint slides. This will allow you to keep all your visual cues in one file during the presentation as opposed to having to toggle between applications.
- **Adult learning (Al).** Providing participants with an opportunity to be self-directed learners is a key element of adult learning theory. Integrating audience response software into a session can provide learners with opportunities to share their thoughts, uncover their needs, and allow you to modify the lesson in the moment as a response.
- **Assessment (As).** Determining whether your learners are "getting it" can be a tricky initiative with smaller groups, and it becomes trickier as your groups grow larger. Asking questions and monitoring responses through audience response software takes some of the pressure off your learners (since their responses are anonymous) while allowing you to determine how many participants can come up with the correct answers to your queries.
- **Virtual meeting (Vm).** If you're conducting a webinar or virtual classroom session, there is software that will integrate with your virtual meeting platform. Most virtual platforms also have built-in polling features that can help you interact with and assess your learners, regardless of the number of participants. Using polling can help break the monotony of virtual lectures and can be an important tool to combat multitasking participants.
- **Instructional design (Id).** While throwing a poll or a survey to your audience from time to time can be a fun way to engage with them, audience response–based activities will always be more powerful when they're designed intentionally into the flow of your program and serve as one element (among many) that helps your learners get to a sufficient level of understanding.

- **Data (Dt).** In addition to relying on traditional evaluation tools such as a smile sheet or other formal assessment, many audience response platforms allow you to download poll results to use as a data point following a session.

A note of caution: Using an audience response tool can be a fun and eye-opening experience for both presenter and participant, but it isn't for the faint of heart. As with any internet-based tool, it is a good idea to make sure you have a back-up plan in place in the event it doesn't behave like you want it to. Internet outages, poor connectivity, finicky computers, or Murphy's Law can derail the best-laid digital audience polling plans. Using voting dots, asking participants to grab a marker and record their vote on a flipchart, or simply having them raise their hands could all be ways to adjust in the event of catastrophic technological meltdowns.

A final note of caution: When you've finished polling, you may want to ask your participants to turn off their devices and put them away, lest they be tempted to check their email.

 ## Element 9
Quiz Software (Qz)

When I was teaching GED classes at the youth center, we'd review the week's content every Friday with a *Jeopardy*-like review game. I had created a gameboard to display in the front of the classroom using a giant, laminated piece of flipchart. While it worked for our purposes, I eventually tried to update my gameboard by transitioning from the flipchart to PowerPoint. This also worked, but it took quite a while to put together all the animation triggers, and every week I had to swap out questions.

In more recent years, I began turning to element 9, Quiz Software. There are many online quizzing platforms—some free, others available on a subscription model—that allow you to quickly turn your content into any number of trivia-style games or quizzes. Honestly, there are so many uses for this element that you're limited only by your imagination (or more realistically, what your organization will allow you to do).

When I worked for one organization, I spoke with our CEO and head of talent management about transforming our monthly all-staff meetings using quiz software. Traditionally, each C-level executive would share high-level departmental metrics from the past month. We experimented with sending out monthly metrics in advance of the all-staff meetings, and then using quiz software to ask all employees—whether they attending the all-staff at our headquarters or joining virtually—to use their smartphones to respond to several high-level questions about each department's monthly performance. It was a more engaging way to focus attention on key statistics for the organization, and it reduced the amount of meeting time we spent listening to executives recapping last month's performance, which freed up time to spend on discussions, interactions, and presentations on current and upcoming initiatives.

While there are many quiz software platforms on the market, this element is typically characterized by:

- Digital-based media (often online, but can also be installed on a local machine)
- Use of a back-end database to track participant scores, which can be accessed at any time

After I've run a session that has incorporated quiz software into the flow of the learning experience, it's become quite common for participants to approach me and say they plan to use the same platform the next time they're in front of their learners. Incorporating quiz software into a training program in an intentional way so you're accomplishing your learning objectives can demonstrate to your learners and your organization what's possible when it comes to a learning experience.

If you are planning to use quiz software in an upcoming session, you may wish to consider bonding it with several other elements:

- **Learning objectives taxonomy (Lo).** What is it that people should be able to do by the end of this session, and does this activity help get us there? These are the questions that should be at the core of any activity you choose for a session, especially one that can generate anxiety. Quizzes, whether they take the form of traditional paper and pencil or a more modern online platform that looks like a game, can generate anxiety. Quiz software can also generate enthusiasm and a sense of competition with some of the game-like offerings available. When you choose to bring this element into your program, it should always align with the learning objectives you've outlined, and you should be sure to let your participants know how their participation can bring them closer to meeting those learning objectives.

- **Instructional design (Id).** While the learning objectives taxonomy is one piece of effective instructional design, you'll want to be sure you've analyzed the needs of your learners, the environment in which you'll be training, and whether or not they'll have the technology necessary to fully benefit from quiz software (it often requires a smartphone or other web-connected device). Is the quiz software a shiny object that would simply be cool and fun to use, perhaps because you've seen it used effectively elsewhere? Or does it fit within the coherent, intentional sequence and flow of a lesson?
- **Data (Dt).** One of the biggest advantages to using quiz software—something it offers much more easily than a flipchart-based or even PowerPoint-based *Jeopardy*-style quiz or review game—is that you can collect individual quiz performance data to analyze whether learners are able to respond accurately to questions about your content. This data can be used for many purposes, such as whether you need to make in-session adjustments to allocate more (or less) time to a specific subject, or as a data point to evaluate how well learners recall specific facts about your content.

Element 10
Google (Gg)

While *search engines* would be the more generic term for this element, I'm using *Google* because in today's common vernacular, not only is Google the name of the most commonly used search engine, but it is also so common that it's turned into a verb used any time someone needs to look something up: Why don't you just google it?

The periodic table of elements found in this book is for "elements of amazing learning experiences." I was careful to not call it a periodic table of "elements of training." Training often implies a learning event that has structure with a beginning and an end and some instruction (and hopefully some activities to explore the content). Learning, on the other hand, implies an ongoing process, often self-directed, and that's where element 10 fits in.

Think back to the last time you needed to learn how to format something in Word or use a specific animation in PowerPoint or create a pivot table in Excel. Did you use Google to figure out the steps in the process? It's likely you did. Or perhaps you needed to figure out a specific setting on your new smartphone or to find a new recipe to dazzle your dinner guests or you wanted to see if you could fix that leaky sink before you spent $250 an hour on a plumber. You could learn how to do any of those things by hopping on Google and running a quick search.

When it comes to search engines such as Google, in the context of amazing learning experiences, there are several distinguishing properties:

- Access to any information publicly available on the internet
- Available in the moment of need

People are learning new things through informal means—including observation, asking questions, trial and error, and, yes, internet searches—all the time. You need not be in a classroom or training room to learn. The more that instructional designers and talent development professionals can come to embrace this fact, the more we can also harness the power of elements like Google to help our learners and organizations.

There will always be a time and place for formal training—whether in the classroom or online—but formal training can never cover everything. Ensuring that learners are encouraged to use resources at their fingertips, such as Google, can alleviate the burden of always having to train people on every piece of content under the sun. In fact, there are times when Google can be used as a substitute for element 40 (instructional design) and can replace formal training sessions.

Adopting a learning strategy that includes the use of search engines aligns perfectly with element 12 (adult learning), which was discussed in much more detail in chapter 1. At a fundamental level, adult learners often thrive in an environment where they can be self-directed. They don't need to constantly be spoon fed; when they have an opportunity to be autonomous and find exactly the information they need at the time in which they need it, they can achieve results in the flow of their regular workday (as opposed to having to be taken offline for formal training, then returning to their work).

Element 11
Video (Vi)

The use of video during a training program can come in all shapes and sizes, from hour-long, professionally produced feature films to homemade, 30-second vignettes filmed with a smartphone.

All training-focused videos share the following common properties:
- Action-based, visual media (as opposed to still photos)
- Flexibility to be used as a standalone resource or integrated into broader learning activities

Using a video in your training program—whether you're creating instructor-led training or asynchronous e-learning experiences—can offer variety to the way in which information is being presented, and can give learners a consistent experience because the video will always be the same.

There are many different types of videos that could serve the purposes of your training program, including:

- **Low-budget, homemade clips.** Video doesn't need to take a lot of time or cost a lot of money to produce. This may be the way to go if you have a smartphone and want to quickly model a certain behavior, capture a specific point using a guest speaker, or demonstrate a process. While smartphone video may not have the editing or lighting necessary to give it that "professional" look and feel, there may be times when you just need to get your point across with a video and a more refined product isn't necessary. I've gone this route on a range of projects, from a CEO welcome message for new employee orientation to a compare-and-contrast set of video clips for effective presentation delivery that was embedded into an e-learning module.

- **Learner-generated.** You should never feel like you have to hold a monopoly on all content and information that can be shared for any type of learning experience. You can ask your learners or colleagues to develop video content you can use during a session, post online, or send as a follow-up to a session. I've had participants record and send clips of their own facilitation as a follow-up to train-the-trainer sessions, and I've also created new employee onboarding programs in which participants had to create a video around a new rule, policy, or piece of organizational culture that they've learned (and which could be played for future groups of new hires).

- **Animation.** As with other types of video, you can generate animation on your own through platforms such as PowToon or Vyond, or an animation can be a professionally produced walk-through of a product, process, or practice. I've seen professionally produced animations used with great effectiveness to demonstrate highly technical content that would be difficult to replicate or demonstrate in the training room.

- **Screen recordings.** You'll read more about screen recording with element 29, but short videos that provide a tutorial for how to navigate a new computer system or show how to navigate a process using a digital application can be extremely helpful. Examples of this can be found using element 49 (YouTube).

- **Interactive.** If you're looking to take your video usage to the next level, then interactive video will bring a new level of engagement to your training program. In the classroom, interactive video could be one where you play a video until a certain point, pause the video, ask participants what they might do in that situation, and then restart the video to see how it actually plays out. In an e-learning environment, interactive video can be viewed as a sort of choose-your-own-adventure learning experience where there are natural pause points in the action and learners are asked to determine what decision should be made in the video. When they make their selection, the video branches and the scenario carries on. This can be done at your desk using software like Camtasia, or you can ask a vendor to work this type of video into your next e-learning project.

- **Professionally produced, off-the-shelf.** Off-the-shelf video options can be extremely expensive and, unfortunately, you don't always get what you pay for. The quality of some off-the-shelf, pre-packaged video can be quite high, almost as if you're watching a corporate version of a made-for-Netflix movie. However, other off-the-shelf video can be kitschy or over the top. The principle of buyer beware definitely applies here. That said, if you can find a high-quality, professionally produced video that aligns with your learning objectives, it can provide a new voice and different media from which your participants can learn.

- **Professionally produced, custom video.** Another option is to work with a video production company. This can be pricey, but if it aligns with your learning objectives and you have the budget, it can really make your training pop. I've worked with vendors to whom I've given a script and shared my general thoughts about the purpose of the video and the learning atmosphere I'm looking to create. They've done the casting and brought in the film crew, lighting, sound equipment, and high-quality cameras. Then they directed the video as I looked on, giving additional in-the-moment suggestions about how the on-set action could ultimately lead to an amazing learning experience.

If video will assist you in accomplishing your learning objectives, it can be used as a substitute for these other elements:

- **Lecture (Lc).** Video that presents your content—by talking about it, demonstrating your concepts in action, or otherwise illustrating your key points—will allow you (or whomever is leading the training session) to take a seat.
- **Subject matter experts (Ex).** Since it can be hard for SMEs to find the time to speak during your session, taking a video of them (or a corporate executive or key organizational influencer) can eliminate the need to coordinate schedules while providing a consistent message during every session. This video can also be used in e-learning content. Recording the SMEs allows you to control the message, ensuring talking points or presentations don't go too long or get off topic.
- **Role play (Rp).** There may be a time and place for role play, but sometimes participants just don't know enough about a topic to effectively navigate simulated situations. Showing a video of two (or more) people navigating your concepts can serve as a model for participants to observe and potentially emulate.

While the use of video elements in a training program can be a stand-alone creation, video also bonds nicely with other elements:

- **Handouts (Hn).** It's not enough to just play the video and assume your learners will focus on the most important parts. Supplying a handout or a page in a participant guide with questions or notetaking prompts can help ensure learners focus on the most salient points.
- **Follow up (Fu).** You can send out links to videos shown in your training program or small video files following each training session to help remind participants about your content or expose them to deeper exploration of ideas just touched upon in your program.
- **E-learning (El).** Video that is integrated into an e-learning module may help break up the monotony of screen after screen of written information. For some e-learning modules, the use of video can be the most dynamic section, illustrating technical procedures or highlighting key concepts in action. Take care with your video size,

however, or it may take your module a while to load. This can be an area of particular sensitivity when distributing e-learning content to learners with internet bandwidth issues.

- **Microlearning (Mc).** Microlearning can come in many forms, and video is one of the most prominent. Offering short clips of a SME speaking or a glimpse of a technical procedure in action can be just enough information for an employee to digest in one sitting so that they're motivated to use your concept or topic to solve a problem.

- **Role play (Rp).** Introducing video into the role play segment of your training program can ensure participants take the simulated situations seriously, because video provides unique insights into their own style and abilities. Asking someone in a small group to use a camera to record a role-play interaction, then asking everyone in the small group to review the role play on video before giving feedback, allows every participant to actually see themselves in action. Were they using the concepts taught in the training session? How is their body language? Did they say "uh" or "um" too much? The camera never lies.

- **Email (Em).** Related to the element of follow up, using email to send video files and clips can help prime your learners for the course (if sent in advance of a training program) or remind themabout key concepts (if sent following a training program).

Element 18
Virtual Meeting (Vm)

Just prior to the COVID-19 outbreak and subsequent quarantine in early 2020, global online print provider Mimeo surveyed L&D professionals who offered sales training on their training delivery methods. Ninety percent of respondents reported that they used instructor-led, face-to-face training, while 64 percent reported delivering training through instructor-led virtual training.

Then the world went on lockdown in an effort to prevent the spread of the virus, which affected all aspects of life, including the way organizations were able to continue developing the skills of their employees. During the pandemic, many organizations decided to go to 100 percent virtual learning, whether synchronous instructor-led or asynchronous e-learning. Virtual training delivery will be with us long after the extreme dangers of COVID-19 have passed, making element 18, virtual meeting platforms, one of the most essential elements on this periodic table.

Here are the fundamental properties of virtual meeting platforms:

- Internet-based software that allows you to conduct meetings and learning experiences from anywhere in the world, with participants who are also located anywhere in the world
- Core capabilities of voice, video, screen share, and text or chat

When deciding to use virtual meeting platforms as part of your overall learning strategy, there are several factors you'll want to keep in mind as you design for maximum engagement:

- **Number of participants.** With fewer participants, there is less need for features. Instead of breakout rooms, you can simply have discussions and conversations with all present. As the group size grows, you'll need to be more thoughtful about how to keep people engaged so that they're not multitasking, checking email, or doing other work during your session. With larger groups, making use of the chat, polling, and breakout room features becomes more important to your design.
- **Degree of technological savvy.** This is one area of virtual delivery that differs greatly from in-person instruction. Some groups may be comfortable with technology while others struggle to log in and locate the chat function. Allocating the first five to 10 minutes of your session to orient participants on the various tools and features you plan to use can be an important way to break the ice and help your participants feel more comfortable with the technology. If you plan to use features such as chat, polling, or on-screen annotation, this would be a good time to set up sample activities and have participants use each feature so that you don't need to take time later on when you're in the flow of your presentation.
- **Duration of the training segment.** Shorter presentations generally mean that you'll be using fewer features, especially more advanced features such as on-screen annotation and breakout rooms. Keep in mind that when you put people into breakout rooms, it takes several minutes simply to adjust to the small-group setting; it may take 10 to 15 minutes for a useful conversation to take place.

- **Platform features.** Remember, not all virtual meeting platforms were created the same. Some are basic and only allow you to use voice or chat functions. Others have all sorts of bells and whistles and allow you to use polling, on-screen annotation, breakout rooms, and quizzes and tests. You'll want to confirm which features are available and active with your IT department as some organizations turn off certain features even though the platform's marketing materials suggest they are available on the platform.

Once you've analyzed the training situation and you know which features of your platform are available to you, you can decide which ones would best connect your learners to the program's learning objectives. Here is a quick overview of features commonly available through virtual meeting platforms:

- **Voice.** You can choose to allow your learners to participate by simply speaking into their microphones. To eliminate distracting background noise, you may wish to ensure everyone is on mute until they have been invited to speak. This will be increasingly important as your group size grows. Otherwise you and your learners may be subjected to dogs barking in the background or side conversations happening in an individual learner's workspace.

- **Video.** Enabling your webcam ensures that participants don't have to simply listen to a bodyless voice throughout the duration of your session. I prefer for everyone to enable their webcams because it's one way to see body language, almost as if we were all together, in person. Another advantage I've found in asking everyone to enable their webcams is that people are generally more present and less likely to multitask if they can be seen by others. While using many of these features may be ideal, keep in mind that it won't always be possible as bandwidth issues, technical difficulties, and cultural or religious objections may prevent some participants from enabling their webcam.

- **Chat.** The chat function can be used in several ways. First, it can be a way to have multiple participants answer questions and engage with your content at the same time, without needing to take people off mute. This is particularly helpful for larger crowds. Some participants simply prefer to type in their thoughts because it seems like a safer way to contribute to the conversation than speaking up and sharing an answer with their voice.

- **Share screen.** Most often, the screen share feature is used by a facilitator to show slides, documents, web pages, videos, or other media. This feature can also be used to invite participants to share their own screens, which is especially helpful when conducting a training session on online systems so the facilitator can see whether a participant is entering information accurately or is competently able to navigate fields and screens.
- **Polling.** Perhaps one of the easiest ways to get your participants to quickly engage with your content, on-screen polls can be set up so that you can gauge your audience's prior knowledge with your topic or to perform knowledge checks to see if your participants are "getting it."
- **On-screen annotation.** It can be helpful to turn control of the content over to your learners. Enabling the on-screen annotation feature in a virtual meeting would be similar to the way in which you can use sticky notes on a flipchart during an in-person session to allow your participants to write their thoughts or brainstorm ideas.
- **Breakout rooms.** Many platforms allow you to put your participants into small groups and send them into breakout rooms. This can raise virtual meeting engagement exponentially by letting participants break into small groups, discuss your content, and then come back into the large group to share themes and thoughts that came up during the small group discussion.
- **Quizzing and testing.** Several platforms allow you to administer quizzes or pre- or post-tests, which can be a convenient way to quickly assess knowledge and retention during your session.

It's one thing to be aware of and familiar with the features available to use during a virtual meeting, but it's another thing to design activities that best take advantage of the features of your platform. Table 4-1 offers some ideas and examples that may be helpful when trying to connect your learning objectives to the features available in your virtual meeting platform.

If you're able to conduct your virtual meeting sessions with a colleague who can serve in a producer role, you'll have a lot more opportunity to focus your time and attention on your content and delivery. A producer is someone with whom you can partner during your session and who can set up and broadcast your polls, monitor the chat for questions, and help participants if they're having technical difficulties. They can also serve as a backup facilitator

Table 4-1. Virtual Training Delivery: Connecting Platform Tools With Learning Objectives

	Voice	Webcam	Screenshare	Chat	Polling	Drawing Tool or Whiteboard	Breakout Rooms	Q&A	Quiz
Explore a new tool or process	•		•	•		•	•		
Use a new tool or process	•	•	•	•		•	•		•
Decide when to use	•		•	•	•	•	•	•	•
Demonstrate the ability	•	•	•	•		•	•		
Measure the impact	•		•	•	•	•			•
List the correct steps in a procedure	•			•		•			•
Articulate a vision	•			•		•	•		
List the components	•		•	•		•			•
Explain the value	•			•			•		•
Justify the use	•			•	•		•		•
Identify a barrier	•			•	•	•	•		•
Develop a plan	•		•	•			•		
Compare and contrast	•			•		•	•		
Identify the implications	•		•	•	•	•	•		•
Evaluate strengths and weaknesses	•		•	•	•	•	•	•	•
Recall information quickly	•			•	•				•
Brainstorm	•		•	•		•	•		
Identify at least three …	•			•	•	•	•	•	•
Prioritize	•			•	•	•	•	•	
Describe the characteristics of	•			•			•	•	
Identify the root causes	•		•	•	•	•	•	•	•
Perform a self-assessment	•	•	•	•	•				•
Perform an assessment	•		•	•	•	•	•		•

in the event you experience catastrophic internet failure (for example, in the event that you are suddenly dropped from the meeting due to a power outage or internet bandwidth issues).

You may wish to bond the use of virtual meeting platforms with some of these other elements:

- **Soapbox (Sb).** While the use of virtual meeting platforms is growing, it can still be difficult to string together a series of activities (beyond just talking at your audience). Soapbox, which you'll explore in more depth later in this chapter, can help generate a sequence and flow of activities customized to the platform you're using.

- **PowerPoint (Pp).** Almost all virtual meetings incorporate PowerPoint as the primary visual aid to walk participants through content. Making sure you're designing your slides to be as engaging and useful as possible will be one key to holding the participants' attention.

- **Dialogue education (De).** Some virtual meetings are designed with the mindset that because people are not all together in the same place, allowing participants to learn through dialogue with one another may not be possible. Nothing can be further from the truth. Incorporating principles of dialogue education, such as safety, praxis, immediacy, teamwork, and learner engagement, is not only possible in a virtual environment, it's also essential.

- **Lesson plan (Lp).** There may be some temptation to open PowerPoint and begin generating slides when you know that you'll be delivering a virtual session, since that will be your primary on-screen visual aid. However, taking the time to completely develop a lesson plan with a sequence and flow of appropriate activities can help ensure your session will run on time and the learning activities do not grow redundant.

- **Icebreakers (Ib).** Since we know that not everyone is comfortable using the technology and features of a virtual meeting platform, try incorporating an icebreaker or two to help your learners grow more comfortable with the features; this can help them get to know the technology, each other, and can be helpful for engagement later in your session.

Element 19
Mr. Sketch Markers (Ms)

I've used Sharpies, Crayola, generic office supply store markers, and when no other option was available to me, I've used dry erase markers to write on a flipchart during a training session. However, I've never found a better flip-chart-focused writing implement than Mr. Sketch markers. This isn't simply a shameless plug; I feel so strongly about this specific marker that I've named a solid element after it. While element 19 could easily be generalized as "markers," the following properties best characterize the unique nature of Mr. Sketch markers:

- Long lasting
- Normal writing will not bleed through to the next flipchart sheet
- Vibrant colors
- Scented

I have no financial interest in Mr. Sketch and haven't done any scientific studies of just how much longer lasting the markers may be, but in my more than 20 years of generating flipcharts, this is certainly what I'd consider to be the premier flipchart writing tool on the market.

The scented nature of this element can also serve to break the ice among learners before a session begins. There have been many occasions during which I've seen participants take their seat, pull off the cap to a Mr. Sketch Marker to make a name tent or create a name tag for themselves, and realize the markers are scented. Inevitably, conversation begins with nearby participants (who they may not have known before they entered the room) asking which scents each person prefers.

While this may seem like a silly thing, finding natural opportunities for participants to engage and interact with one another prior to a session helps lower anxiety levels that may be natural for many people entering into a new, formal situation such as an in-person training session. When anxiety is reduced, the likelihood of learning increases.

For maximum results when using Mr. Sketch markers, you may wish to bond this element with one or more of the following:

- **Lecture (Lc).** While key points listed on PowerPoint slides often accompany traditional lecture, you can make lecture more dynamic by writing key points on a flipchart or capturing learners' thoughts, which can make a lecture more interactive as well.
- **Dialogue education (De).** As you'll discover in more depth in the next chapter, Jane Vella's concept of dialogue education is based on the idea that learners thrive when instruction comes through dialogue. Having opportunities to discuss ideas, concepts, and content in small groups; capture them on a flipchart; and then report back to the large group is another way to integrate Mr. Sketch markers into an amazing learning experience.

133

- **Flipchart (Fc).** If you're not using Mr. Sketch markers to write on name tents or to make a name tag, then it seems capturing thoughts on a flipchart is the most logical and most frequent use of Mr. Sketch Markers. That said, if you're conducting an activity in which participants are brainstorming thoughts on sticky notes and then sticking those notes onto a flipchart at the front of the room, using Mr. Sketch markers would be easier to read by more people than if your learners use pens or finer-tipped markers.
- **Games (Ga).** Asking participants to grab a Mr. Sketch marker and quickly write one idea, reflection, or concept on a series of flipcharts posted around the room in a sort of "write-n-run" activity can bring the energy up in your room while getting participants involved in generating content or sharing their thoughts. There are a variety of ways to structure review-style games using Mr. Sketch markers and flipcharts to start your day, close out an activity, or wrap up the session.

Element 20
Flipchart (Fc)

An old-fashioned easel and giant pad of paper can keep things simple in the training room, but the value of a flipchart is often understated. First, let's talk about the key properties of this element:

- Pad of oversized paper
- Flexibility allows for sheets to remain on the easel, be torn off and used by individuals or groups, and be posted on the wall of a training room

Flipcharts offer several benefits in the training room that can't be replicated by PowerPoint or other digital visual aids. First, when a PowerPoint slide is advanced during a session, it's gone. You're on to your next point. A flipchart page, on the other hand, when posted on the wall of a training room, is there for your participants to look at for the remainder of your session. Second, it democratizes the training room by allowing participants to capture their own thoughts and share their experiences with the rest of the cohort, which sometimes generates content the trainer wouldn't have even thought to mention.

While some people prefer to simply write on a flipchart as the need arises, some of the following suggestions offer ways to leverage this element to ensure an amazing learning experience.

- **Prepare in advance when possible.** Neatness counts, and it shows your participants that you've taken the time to ensure a crisp, organized learning environment. Revealing a pre-made flipchart page during your session helps you look organized and in control of the sequence and flow of your program. Trying to scribble out some thoughts in the moment has a time and place, but it shouldn't happen all the time.

- **You don't need to be artistic.** In fact, you don't need to write on them at all. I've worked with many colleagues who ask someone else in their office to prepare their flipcharts in advance. I've worked with others who have had their artistically inclined children help them out. Even if you don't have someone you can turn to, don't stress about it. People probably aren't coming to your training session for your artistic abilities. Capture your key points and then focus on your delivery.

- **Economize on words and write big.** Just like with PowerPoint slides, there's no need to write complete sentences or even complete thoughts on the flipchart. Use fewer words and write big enough so that the people in the back of the room can see what you've written.

- **Use the pencil trick.** Even though you shouldn't write out your whole presentation in marker and you really should economize on the words your learners can see on your flipchart, it doesn't mean you can't use a pencil to lightly write out your talking points on the flipchart to provide a reminder of everything you want to say when you're standing close enough to your giant piece of paper.

- **Use appropriate markers.** Dry erase markers will dry out quickly if you use them on flipchart paper. Many permanent markers will bleed through to the next page. Lighter colors become very difficult to see (but they're useful for shading if you happen to be drawing images). As you might be able to tell from element 19, I recommend using Mr. Sketch markers.

- **Alternate colors.** When you're making lists, it's helpful to use two different colors in an alternating fashion so that your learners can tell when one point ends and another begins. Use care with your color combinations as some participants may be colorblind and will not be able to distinguish between some pairings.

- **Bring painter's tape or wall mounting putty.** Some people responsible for facilities—whether in your office or in hotel meeting rooms—do not like you to use tape to affix something to the walls. There are a lot of flipcharts available nowadays that come with adhesive already applied to the back of each sheet. However, if you're using a flipchart that is not sticky, you may need to pick up a roll of blue painter's tape (which comes off the wall much easier—good for the facilities people, but not always good for holding your Flipcharts to the wall for the entire day) or the mounting putty teenagers use to put up posters in their bedrooms.
- **Make sure you know when to use them.** While flipcharts can be extremely useful, it's not an effective visual medium in certain situations. In large hotel ballrooms, for example, it can be very difficult for participants to see a flipchart in the front of the room or posted on the wall. In situations where you are generating ideas and promise participants you'll send that list out after your training session, you may want to take notes in a Word document that is projected onto a screen. This can save you a lot of post-training work when it comes to transcribing those ideas to send them out.

With some of these helpful hints and ideas in mind, you can use this element as a substitute for several other commonly (over)used elements on our periodic table, including:

- **Audience response (Re).** If you want to know how your participants feel about something, how much they know about something, or if you simply want them to cast a vote during your session, then giving them small, round voting dot stickers and asking them to place them on a flipchart can be a quick, analogue alternative to audience response software.
- **PowerPoint (Pp).** I've delivered multi-day train-the-trainer and presentation skills courses without the use of a single PowerPoint slide to illustrate that you don't need to use PowerPoint to have an effective, engaging session. While you don't need to take things to my extreme on a regular basis, being able to add a visual element using flipcharts in the front of the room or posted around the room can keep key concepts in front of your learners for the duration of your training session.

- **Handouts (Hn).** There are times when key points are distributed to your learners in the form of pre-printed handouts. If your participants won't need those key points after the session, you can save some trees by eliminating that handout and simply using a prepared flipchart page.

When you've chosen to bring flipcharts into a training session, you may wish to forge bonds with one or more of the following elements:

- **Soapbox (Sb).** Any time you generate a training session using Soapbox, which is a software tool you'll read about in more depth later in this chapter, you'll want to have a tablet of flipchart paper available. Soapbox takes some basic information about your presentation and quickly generates activities designed to engage your audience, such as small group discussions or group brainstorming. Other Soapbox-generated activities, such as the gallery walk or a poster session, will ask that the trainer or the participants generate content on a flipchart page and post it on the wall. Then everyone will be asked to file past the series of exhibits or posters around the room, noting key concepts or content.
- **Lecture (Lc).** One way to make a traditional lecture more dynamic is to write key points on a flipchart as they are brought up, helping focus participant attention on the salient information.
- **Adult learning (Al).** Allowing participants the opportunity to discuss concepts in small groups, capture a summary of those discussions on a flipchart, and then present back to the larger group is one way to honor the autonomous nature of adult learners.
- **Lesson plan (Lp).** Clearly marking which activities require a flipchart will ensure you know when and how to use this element when the time comes during your session.
- **Mr. Sketch markers (Ms).** Be sure you have the correct writing instrument to create vivid imagery and bold print on your flipchart so your learners take away your key points.
- **Visual design (Vd).** While you don't have to be an artist to use a flipchart, it doesn't mean you should scribble your way through the use of this element. Carefully laying out key points, content, and images will help your learners process the information more easily.

Element 27
Rapid Authoring (Ra)

The first time I rolled out an e-learning project, my (small-budget nonprofit) organization paid a media company upwards of $75,000 for a module that was developed and coded from scratch. Despite the highly successful end result, the days of needing to pay a media company so much money for a custom-coded module are gone. The rise of rapid authoring tools such as Articulate Storyline and Adobe Captivate have made it easy for in-house talent and inexpensive e-learning contractors to quickly develop modules that, not too long ago, would have cost tens or hundreds of thousands of dollars and taken months to develop.

Rapid authoring tools share the following characteristics:
- Software that is easily accessible to the general public
- An interface that is familiar and intuitive
- Allows for content to be generated and published to the internet or an LMS
- Does not require advanced coding skills

While the element of rapid authoring tools has been classified as a solid and not a radioactive element, its ease of use and wide availability do pose a danger. Just like PowerPoint has opened the door to a lot of bad instructor-led training because it has been used so poorly by so many for so long, rapid authoring tools can also be abused in the name of quickly generated content and e-learning. It is possible to simply generate a bunch of screens of content (think about something that resembles a long PowerPoint deck with slide after slide of information), press the "Publish to LMS" button, and voila, you have a long, boring, "click-through" e-learning module.

On the other hand, there are a lot of advantages to using rapid authoring software to create e-learning modules. With a little bit of training, reading, experimenting, or interacting with your preferred software's online community, it's possible to generate choose-your-own-adventure–style, scenario-based learning, simulations, games, and feature-rich content.

For example, Articulate calls its online community the "E-learning Heroes Community" and features a blog with tips, tricks, hacks, and short-cuts; a weekly e-learning challenge to test your budding development skills and to see what kinds of creative ideas other users can come up with; and an extremely active membership who share their own work samples and provide quick answers for user questions. Figures 4-3 and 4-4 show how leveraging an online community can help you to quickly develop better learning experiences.

In this first example, anyone new to these tools can ask basic questions to quickly get started (Figure 4-3).

Figure 4-3. Asking Basic Questions for Support

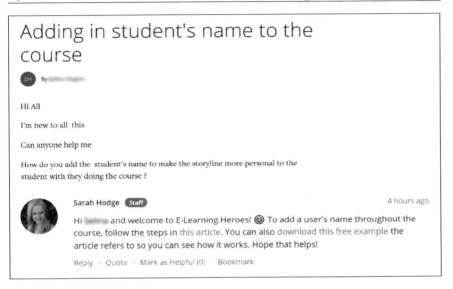

Even more experienced, advanced users can leverage the online community to work on their skills and ensure their design doesn't grow stale (Figure 4-4).

The key with rapid authoring (or any other element on this periodic table) is that for best use, we need to continue to find new, better, more advanced ways to bring them to life. Failure to do this will result in learning experiences that eventually appear out of date or, worse, that no longer align with best practices in learning design.

Because rapid authoring tools are a primary means of generating e-learning content, there are a whole host of elements to consider bonding with your next online module project:

- **Video (Vi).** As mentioned earlier in this chapter, video in the form of a technical expert, an animation to illustrate a process, or an interactive experience that branches in different directions based upon a learner's

Figure 4-4. Leveraging an Online Community as an Expert User

Using Hotspots and Invisible Buttons in E-Learning #296

Hotspots are interactive objects that work a lot like regular buttons. They can show layers, change states, jump to slides, and do almost everything standard buttons can do. What makes hotspots so unique is they're invisible buttons.

Because they're invisible, you can test learners' ability to identify parts of an image without providing hints or guides for the learner. To help you out in working with hotspots, Storyline displays the hotpots as transparent green shapes.

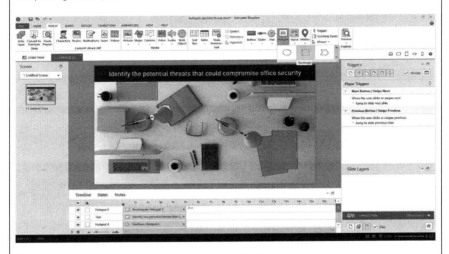

Click-and-reveal interactions are just one use case for hotspots.

Hotspots can control sorting order and drop targets in custom drag-and-drop interactions. They can be used as transparent barriers to prevent learners from clicking other objects on the slide. What else can you do with hotspots? That's what this week's challenge is all about!

Challenge of the Week

This week, your challenge is to show how hotspots and invisible buttons can be used in e-learning.

Never used hotspots? No problem. You can learn all about them in our user guide: Working with Hotspots.

Share Your E-Learning Work

- **Comments:** Use the comments section below to share a link to your published example and blog post.

- **Forums:** Start your own thread and share a link to your published example.

- **Personal blog:** If you have a blog, please consider writing about your challenges. We'll link back to your posts so the great work you're sharing gets even more exposure.

- **Social Media:** If you share your demos on Twitter or LinkedIn, try using #ELHChallenge so your tweeps can track your e-learning coolness.

Source: Anderson (2020).

response can all help to break up the monotony of clicking "Next" to get to the subsequent screen.

- **Handouts (Hn).** Most rapid authoring tools allow you to upload resources, job aids, manuals, and other materials that can be downloaded or printed for reference after an e-learning module has been completed.
- **Screen capture (Sc).** If you're going to include images of software or other visuals that can be lifted from your computer screen, then ensuring you have a clear, crisp image by way of high- quality screen capture tools can help ensure your learner can see what you need them to see.
- **Screen recording (Sr).** There are times when an explainer video that demonstrates the steps to a process or where to click on a screen is more effective than still photos. Uploading short videos using screen recording software can help learners see how a process should flow. Be sure to add video controls to your interface if this is something you plan to use so that your learners can pause and restart the video as necessary.
- **Visual design (Vd).** By its nature, e-learning is a visual experience. Using rapid authoring software to develop e-learning modules quickly and inexpensively doesn't mean that you should ignore basic visual design concepts. Be sure to determine the type of device on which learners will be navigating the module (the visual design and functionality will be different if learners are using a phone and need to tap in certain places compared with using a computer and being able to use a mouse to navigate). In addition, it's important to use consistency with placement of buttons, font choices, color schemes, and screen layout. A haphazard visual design can lead to a frustrating learning experience.
- **Microlearning (Mc).** Short videos may be the most common thing that comes to mind when you think of microlearning, but rapid authoring tools can help you put together very short, focused e-learning modules that put the exact right amount of information into the hands of your learners and employees in their time of need.
- **Learning objectives taxonomy (Lo).** Defining exactly what your learners should be able to do by the end of your e-learning module can help make sure you're using the appropriate features of your rapid

authoring tool. If you want your learners to be able to list the steps to a process, many rapid authoring tools allow you to create blank fields in which learners can type those steps; or perhaps you'd prefer to use a drag-and-drop style activity. If you want your learners to demonstrate their ability to suggest the appropriate product to their customer, you may want to use your rapid authoring tool's feature for triggers, branching, and layers to create scenarios and provide feedback based upon the choices your learners make.

- **Games (Ga).** When you grow more comfortable in your abilities to use a rapid authoring tool, you can begin to develop e-learning elements that mimic popular video games such as *Angry Birds* or game shows such as *Jeopardy* or *Press Your Luck*. These add a degree of levity, fun, and engagement that help meet your learning objectives while keeping learners interested and attentive.

Element 28
Screen Capture (Sc)

Did you know that the PrtSc key on your computer's keyboard can capture the image that's on your monitor? It's a neat shortcut, and there are many other ways to capture high-quality images of something on your screen if you plan to use it for training purposes.

Screen capture software is just as it sounds—it enables you to take a picture of an image that's on your screen or monitor. These are the most prominent properties of this element:

- Takes still images of all or a portion of what appears on your computer screen
- Saves the image for use as-is or so you can manipulate it to meet your training needs

Many operating systems come with a snipping tool already installed (you may need to search your pre-installed software to find it) and other products on the market, such as TechSmith's Snagit, are also commonly used to capture still images. Some screen capture software allows you to make edits or superimpose things (for example, text, markers, or arrows to draw attention to a specific feature of your image), while other software will require you to save your image and then use photo-editing software to do that manipulation.

In some instances, screen capture images can be printed, laminated, and left as standalone job aids. I worked in one office where our office manager took a series of screen captures, superimposed a few instructions over the images, and left them in each conference room so that people didn't have to keep asking her for assistance in connecting their devices to the projector. More often, however, screen capture imagery can be quite effective when bonded to any of these other elements:

- **Word (Wd).** While I offered the example of some images being left in a conference room, oftentimes job aids require a little more context. Building user manuals or quick reference guides will rely in part on high-quality images. Embedding those images into a Word document so that you have space to write more detailed instructions or steps in a process can be important to assist people in more complex tasks.

- **PowerPoint (Pp).** Some medical professionals use screen capture to get imagery from microscopes or other medical equipment connected to a camera. Some training professionals embed screen capture images from software tools and databases to assist in new user orientation for those systems. Regardless of your topic, if you have real-life images of your concepts or processes to share, you can use them to break up the text on your PowerPoint slides.

- **Learning boosts (Lb).** Following a training session, it can be beneficial to send quick reference materials, helpful hints, or shortcuts using screen capture imagery to solidify your learners' retention and improve their ability to apply what you've taught them.

- **Quiz software (Qz).** If you're looking to assess your learners' understanding of topics such as software usage and navigation, then posing a screen capture image and asking people to identify specific fields or explain the order in which a screen should be navigated can replace traditional text-based quiz questions and make the assessment more true-to-life.

- **E-learning (El).** When it comes to system training, you can recreate screens or pages in a system by taking screen capture images and overlaying clickable hotspots to provide learners an opportunity to practice navigating a system and give them feedback if they aren't clicking in the right areas.

Element 29
Screen Recording (Sr)

A cross between elements 11 (video) and 28 (screen capture), screen recording software is a specific tool that allows you to record what's happening on your monitor in real-time to create short video tutorials or explainer videos that can range from navigating software and computer-based systems to simply walking people through an automated narration of your slide deck. While there are a variety of free and fee-based tools available, including Camtasia, Screencast-o-Matic, iMovie, and Windows Moviemaker, the principal properties that any screen recording software share include:

- Records live-action images on your screen, including the movement of your mouse
- Records voice narration while navigating the images on your screen

Some screen recording software also allows you to edit your video, publish to the internet, or save the video to your local drive.

Screen recordings can serve as stand-alone resources that provide short, on-demand bursts of information in the moment of need (also known as microlearning, which you can explore in more detail by turning to element 35), but they can also be important components of larger learning programs when bonded with any of the following elements:

- **Learning boosts (Lb).** Keep in mind that your learners won't remember everything about your content, steps in a process, or the software program on which you've just finished training them. Sending short video tutorials to remind them about what they learned or that feature advanced tips and tricks can refresh their memories and recharge their desire to use what they've learned.

- **Subject matter experts (Ex).** There may be times when an expert in the topic you'd like to expose your learners to isn't available on a regular basis. Asking that person to walk through their slides while narrating key concepts can become a much more helpful resource than simply distributing a PowerPoint deck on its own. Screen recording software allows an expert to pull up their slide deck, advance through their slides, and talk about their key points as if they were giving a presentation; you can then distribute the recording to the masses.

- **Spaced learning (Sl).** Similar to learning boosts, some concepts, processes, or software tools are complex and require practice and exposure over time. You may wish to queue up a series of short video recordings to distribute to your learners as part of a drip campaign that will expose them to a series of tutorials and informative videos over the course of days, weeks, or months.
- **E-learning (El).** Whether you produce a video tutorial to show your employees how to access your LMS or you embed screen-based tutorials in your learning program, offering screen recordings provides a more dynamic way to present information in your e-learning modules.
- **Collaborative file sharing (Cf).** Having text-based user guides to navigate organizational systems isn't always enough. Sometimes you just need a widely accessible library of video tutorials that can help your employees perform certain functions or find out how to complete and submit an expense form.
- **YouTube (Yt).** Some organizations have a private YouTube channel; some people may work with external audiences. Either way, if you want to broadcast and promote the screen-based video content you've produced, YouTube can be a simple-to-use platform to house your content and distribute links that anyone will be able to access.

Element 36
Soapbox (Sb)

"Wouldn't it be cool if we could create an app that just made it easy for anyone—even if they didn't have an instructional design background—to generate engaging training that led to behavior change?" It was a comment I made over breakfast with a friend at a Washington, DC, diner. Several years later, the youngest element on the Periodic Table of Amazing Learning Experiences was born.

A closer look at the properties of Soapbox reveals that it's a web-based tool that:

- Is designed to be used for instructor-led training (whether in-person or virtual)
- Generates a lesson plan with a sequence and flow of training activities connected to your learning objectives

Soapbox is a tool for learning and development professionals to save time and generate a high-quality learning experience, although—as with all the elements on this periodic table—you'll reap an amount of benefits commensurate with how much time you put in to mastering the best time and place for its use.

When experimenting with this element, you may need several minutes to generate a basic set of learning activities. You can always choose to spend additional time refining what's been generated. Soapbox takes some basic information about your session (the duration of your presentation, anticipated number of attendees, your learning objectives, and whether you're delivering an in-person session or virtual session) and generates a series of learning activities. You'll then need to add talking points or technical information to the lesson plan it generates for you.

Soapbox is an interesting element because it automates several key pieces of the instructional design process (which we discussed in chapter 1, element 40). Using Soapbox in some situations can actually allow you to substitute or eliminate the need to have deep knowledge of the following elements:

- **Adult learning (Al).** Knowledge of or familiarity with the key principles of adult learning is absolutely encouraged for anyone who plans to be in front of a room teaching new concepts, skills, or practices to groups of adults. Of course, presentations can also be successful when delivered by people who have limited or no knowledge of adult learning. Soapbox generates presentations that are designed to connect all learning activities with the intended learning outcomes, which naturally yields relevance to the learning experience and helps learners identify ways in which the content will solve problems they may be facing.
- **Dialogue education (De).** Dialogue education, examined in more depth in chapter 1, is a practice grounded in the idea that learners thrive through engaged exploration of concepts and conversation. Through the use of anchor activities (which help participants connect their own experiences to the content about to be presented) and application activities (which provide an opportunity to more deeply explore the day's content through discussion, role play, or simulations), the plans generated by Soapbox encourage participants to learn through dialogue with the facilitator as well as their fellow learners.

- **Lesson plan (Lp).** As you learned with the first element in this chapter, a well-designed lesson plan includes an outline of the sequence and flow of activities, along with activity instructions and talking points for your key content. Soapbox generates a facilitator guide, which eliminates the need to be familiar with how to create a lesson plan on your own.
- **Instructional design (Id).** Oftentimes when we ask subject matter experts or nontraining colleagues to present, we hope (or expect) them to appreciate and apply some of the finer points of instructional design to come up with a training session that is somehow engaging. Soapbox generates a training session that incorporates key principles of instructional design to engage the audience through a series of relevant activities, eliminating the need for nontrainers to spend time learning about instructional design and reducing the time needed for training professionals to come up with creative ways to engage their audience.

If you plan to use the element of Soapbox to develop amazing learning experiences, you may wish to bond it with one or more of these elements:

- **Subject matter experts (Ex).** While Soapbox makes it easy to come up with a logical sequence and flow of activities, you will still need to fill in your own content. Using your own knowledge or engaging a subject matter expert to determine key talking points, technical data, or other content-related information can round out anything generated by Soapbox.
- **Mr. Sketch markers (Ms).** Many of the activities generated by Soapbox—from setting up stations around the room with pre-made posters for small-group discussion to fast-paced games to get your participants out of their seats—will require the use of flipcharts and markers. As I've mentioned already, the most solid of writing instruments (in my opinion) is the Mr. Sketch marker.
- **Flipchart (Fc).** When you use Soapbox you'll often be employing activities that require writing or call for voting dots or sticky notes to be prominently displayed. Flipcharts are a great resource for these activities.
- **Smile sheets (Sm).** Post-training evaluation forms allow you to collect information about your participants' reactions to any learning

experience in which you choose to use training tools, such as Soapbox. It's especially important to collect as many data points as possible when you employ a new tool or element for your learning program.

- **Virtual meeting (Vm).** As we discussed earlier in this chapter, just because you're planning to deliver a virtual session doesn't mean you shouldn't take the same care and intentionality that you would when designing in-person training. In fact, it can be trickier to come up with activities that engage your virtual learners and lead to effective training. Soapbox can help you generate a virtual learning experience with appropriate activities that help keep your learners engaged while aligning with your learning outcomes.

Element 37
Collaborative File Sharing (Cf)

Many organizations have central repositories of information, resources, policies, and other internal materials that are collaboratively stored somewhere employees across the organization can access. Some common collaborative file sharing platforms include SharePoint, Google Drive, OneDrive, or internal wiki sites. Regardless of the platform used, the collaborative file sharing element is characterized by the following properties:

- Central knowledge repository
- Accessible across the organization
- Dynamic platform allowing for a variety of people to continually share knowledge and update with new information or resources

Remember, not every element in the Periodic Table of Amazing Learning Experiences must be applied to formal learning design (whether *formal* to you means instructor-led learning or e-learning). People are learning all the time, all day long; however, sharing organizational knowledge through an up-to-date collaborative file sharing system is also a way to harness institutional memory and put key information and resources at a learner's fingertips in their moment of need.

Self-proclaimed learning geek JD Dillon explains that too many organizational learning strategies are built around a "training-first" mentality (Figure 4-5).

He created a framework for a Modern Learning Ecosystem, which is built upon a foundation of shared knowledge that leans heavily upon the element of collaborative file sharing (Figure 4-6).

Figure 4-5. The Training-First Mentality: Unbalanced Ecosystem

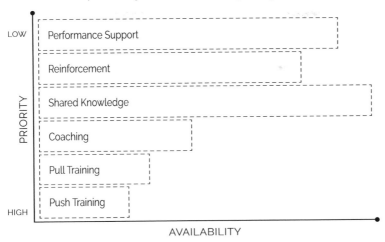

Organizations that base their learning strategy on a foundation of formal, push training create an unbalanced, rigid ecosystem.

Figure 4-6. The Modern Learning Ecosystem Framework

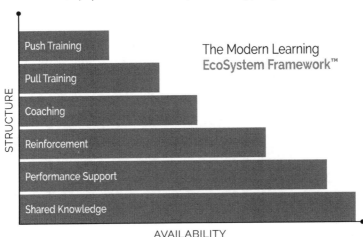

The MLE Framework realigns familiar tactics based on the realities of the employee workflow as well as proven learning principles.

While this is not intended to be a book that goes deeply into organizational learning strategy, if you remember nothing else about elements 10 (Google) and 37 (collaborative file sharing), remember that not all learning needs to be done in a formal way. Offering guidance and leveraging organizational tools and platforms to share knowledge can offer people around your organization an opportunity to learn exactly what they need, when they need it, 24 hours a day.

Element 38
Text Tools (Tt)

How many unread emails do you have in your inbox at any given moment? Now think about how many unread text messages you have. My guess is that you read your text messages with much more immediacy than you do your emails.

For that reason, element 38 can be a powerful way to distribute content or remind people about your topic. Using text tools can also be a controversial element if it's not implemented with care because some learners may decry it as an invasion of their personal space.

The element text tools is characterized by:

- SMS-based technology
- Distribution of content, website links, or quiz questions to learners

The way text tools work is that you use a software program to load small bursts of content, relevant links to web pages, or a short series of quiz questions (sometimes you just need one question) and then you push that content, link, or quiz out to your learners via text message.

Since many learners carry SMS-enabled devices, this element can easily deliver information to them in the flow of their daily routine. In fact, in areas where internet bandwidth is spotty or nonexistent, this is not just a nice-to-have tool, it can sometimes be the only means of delivering content, at scale, over large geographic regions. This is especially important to keep in mind when an estimated 3.8 billion people on this planet (many of them in the developing world) are not connected to the internet at all (ITU 2020).

While text messaging may be a convenient, direct line to learners, it may also be a little too convenient. Before you choose to push information out this way, you'll want to be sure you have permission from your learners (text messaging has long been considered someone's personal space) and their organization (pushing work-related material to someone's personal device can violate organizational policies and may require employees to be compensated for work that is performed outside normal working hours).

While there are examples of entire courses being built using text tools, this element can be enhanced when it is bonded with:

- **Learning boosts (Lb).** Well-timed text messages to remind participants of your content, point them toward job aids, or augment what they've studied are all examples of how text tools can be leveraged to boost retention and adoption of new concepts.
- **Assessment (As).** Post-testing at the end of a training program can yield a data point that isn't necessarily an indicator of learning or retention because little time will have passed between the end of instruction and the time learners take the test. Using text tools to send several quiz questions in the days or weeks following a learning experience can offer a more realistic indicator of how much your learners have actually retained.
- **Microlearning (Mc).** Providing small bites of information via SMS may be all your learners need.
- **Learning objectives taxonomy (Lo).** Regardless of the actual content you plan to push to your learners, it's important to ask yourself: Will sending this text message help my learners demonstrate their ability to do something new, differently, or better? In other words, will it help accomplish the learning objectives that have been established for this experience?
- **Instructional design (Id).** Putting together a coherent campaign of messages will depend on how well you've analyzed the needs of your learners and their ability to use their device, as well as how well you put together and execute the messaging and distribution of engaging, relevant content.

Reflection: Useful Tool or Shiny Object?

You've just examined 15 tools that you can use to more easily (or creatively) put together an engaging, effective training program. Now you need to ask yourself: Should you use one or more of these tools? Or are some (or all) of these tools merely shiny objects? Perhaps the answer to these questions is, "It depends on the situation."

Using Table 4-2, take some time to reflect on whether some or all of these tools would be right for you, and in which scenario they might work best, based on your current working environment, culture, and available resources.

Element	Where would this element serve as a solid tool for developing a more effective, engaging learning experience? How?	Is it a shiny object?
Lesson Plan (Lp)		
Word (Wd)		
Audience Response (Re)		
Quiz Software (Qz)		
Google (Gg)		
Video (Vi)		
Virtual Meeting (Vm)		
Mr. Sketch Markers (Ms)		
Flipchart (Fc)		
Rapid Authoring (Ra)		
Screen Capture (Sc)		
Screen Recording (Sr)		
Soapbox (Sb)		
Collaborative File Sharing (Cf)		
Text Tools (Tt)		

Chapter 5
Interactive Elements

Tw	Li	Bl	Wb	Yt	Sh	Em
Twitter	LinkedIn	Blog	Website	YouTube	Slideshare	Email

Amazing learning experiences don't always happen in a formal setting.

Several years ago, a colleague, Michelle Baker, and I put our heads together to pitch and write an article in *TD* magazine. We brainstormed ideas, took turns writing, and eventually produced a finished product.

About a year after that article was published, another colleague, Mike Taylor, and I put our heads together to propose and design a workshop at *Training* magazine's Online Learning Conference.

Both of these were fairly big, intense, involved projects. Yet, by the time we had finished, I'd still never actually met Michelle or Mike in person.

Michelle and I wrote personal, training-related blogs. At some point, we reached out to each other and connected, co-writing blogs and eventually writing and publishing the article. Mike and I found each other on Twitter, interacted through a number of chats, and then decided we could team up on a conference presentation.

Herein is the power of interactive elements. While many of the elements outlined in the periodic table at the core of this book offer thoughts and ideas about how to create amazing learning experiences through formal, structured training programs, the elements in this chapter lead to much less formal (but no less powerful) learning experiences.

Of course, when you begin to experiment with any sort of formula involving interactive elements, who knows what kind of power you can unleash.

What Are Interactive Elements?

Introducing interactive elements from social media into a learning experience is a way you can prime learners in advance for a course. You can also use these elements to keep the learning experience going, such as through hosting blogs on a blogging (Bl) site, posting slides on SlideShare (Sh), or challenging participants to participate in a topical chat via Twitter (Tw).

There are seven interactive elements: Twitter (Tw), LinkedIn (Li), blog (Bl), website (Wb), YouTube (Yt), SlideShare (Sh), and email (Em). Using these interactive elements requires a degree of daring and trust, because there can be a disconnect between you and the learners. Typically, these elements are used outside the a formal classroom, which means you need to give up an element of control.

Several organizations I've worked with use Mailchimp to automatically send out emails (Em) with learning boosts (Lb; see liquid elements) following a training session to aid learners in retaining key concepts and content. Some conference organizers invite attendees to write guest posts reflecting on their key learnings and experiences, and then publish them on the organization's blog (Bl) in the days and weeks after their conference.

When you introduce interactive elements into a learning strategy, you're all but guaranteeing that learning will be more than just a one-way experience. Because of social media's broad reach, learners can reply to the trainer, other learners, or the world at large (thus the label: *interactive* elements).

As you take a look at the interactive elements listed on the periodic table, you may find that your social media platform of choice has been left out. The elements here are not meant to be an all-encompassing list of platforms, but hopefully the descriptions and examples surrounding them will offer transferable lessons and inspire you to find ways to integrate your preferred social media platform as appropriate into your next learning experience.

If you do plan to incorporate interactive elements into a learning program, you'll want to be sure your design ideas align with the platform's format. Using Twitter (Tw) may be good for very short bursts of information, links, images, or just connecting people with one another, but it wouldn't be an appropriate platform if you'd like to write in-depth, detailed articles for your learners. YouTube (Yt) would be the perfect element when directing learners to video, but if you wanted to offer more context around the video, perhaps you'll want to leverage a blog (Bl) or website (Wb) in which you can embed video while surrounding it with text. For this reason, you may want to take particular note of the properties of each interactive element.

Element 45
Twitter (Tw)

Twitter is an online social media platform perhaps best known for providing a forum for short bursts of information or commentary. Several of the core properties of this platform include:

- Short-form (there used to be a 140-character limit on messages, and though that limit has been lifted it remains a microblogging site)
- Posts may be public (anyone who follows you or looks at your profile can see them) or private
- Use of hashtags allows you to filter or search for keywords and information
- You can create groups to better organize Twitter accounts that you follow

Although Twitter has made the news in recent years for the way in which it is leveraged by celebrities and politicians, it also commonly falls among the top 10 in the Centre for Learning and Performance Technologies' annual survey of the top 200 tools for learning. Let's look at five ways you may wish to leverage Twitter:

- **Resources galore.** Whether you're researching articles, podcasts, or blog posts that align with your content or directing your learners to additional information, Twitter is crawling with learning professionals who are eager to share. If you find information to be reputable, you can amplify it by passing it along to your learners or retweeting it for the rest of the world to see. (Just be smart. There's a lot of information out there, but not all of it is evidence- or research-based.)
- **Live interaction with the broader learning community.** Twitter chats are live, Twitter-based, facilitated interactions that typically happen on a regular basis, often sponsored by a group or organization. Figure 5-1 shows an example of the interaction from #guildchat, which is a Twitter chat that takes place on Fridays. Because these Twitter chats often occur on a regular schedule, you may wish to block them off on your calendar or assign them to participants as part of a learning program. However, be sure to let your supervisor know that these are actual learning opportunities lest your boss walk by and think you're just playing around!

Figure 5-1. Example Twitter Chat

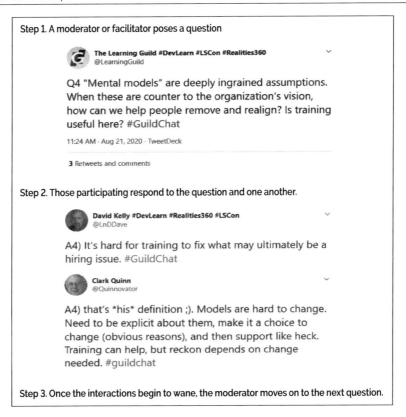

Step 1. A moderator or facilitator poses a question

> **The Learning Guild #DevLearn #LSCon #Realities360**
> @LearningGuild
>
> Q4 "Mental models" are deeply ingrained assumptions. When these are counter to the organization's vision, how can we help people remove and realign? Is training useful here? #GuildChat
>
> 11:24 AM · Aug 21, 2020 · TweetDeck
>
> **3** Retweets and comments

Step 2. Those participating respond to the question and one another.

> **David Kelly #DevLearn #Realities360 #LSCon**
> @LnDDave
>
> A4) It's hard for training to fix what may ultimately be a hiring issue. #GuildChat

> **Clark Quinn**
> @Quinnovator
>
> A4) that's *his* definition ;). Models are hard to change. Need to be explicit about them, make it a choice to change (obvious reasons), and then support like heck. Training can help, but reckon depends on change needed. #guildchat

Step 3. Once the interactions begin to wane, the moderator moves on to the next question.

- **Connecting with thought leaders.** I have found no easier way to connect with thought leaders in the field of learning and development than through following and engaging with them on Twitter. As you can see from Figure 5-1, many thought leaders participate in industry conversations, and Twitter offers ample opportunities for quality interactions.

- **Establishing a personal learning network (PLN).** Having access to like-minded people who are passionate about the field of learning and development is important for ongoing professional development. While this may seem especially true for people who work in small departments (or are a "team of one"), it's also true for those who work in large organizations. Twitter offers the opportunity for exposure to new ideas, trends, and tools that others are using. As I mentioned at the start of this chapter, I've collaborated with people whom I'd never met in person to work on blog posts, conference presentations, and magazine articles. Twitter makes the world a much smaller place and provides endless opportunities to build relationships with and learn from others in the field on an ongoing basis.

- **Live tweeting.** Some learners need to write down key points they're learning to help them remember certain concepts. In the "olden days," this happened using a pen and paper, and those notes were kept private. With Twitter, conference session attendees and training participants can not only take notes, but they can share those notes with others who were unable to attend a session. When they attach a hashtag to those notes, often corresponding to the conference, learning event, or topic, the rest of the world can easily search for and find highlights from a variety of learning events.

While there are probably infinite other ways you can leverage Twitter to up your learning and development game, if you'd like to bring this interactive element into your learning programs, you may wish to bond it with one or more of the following:

- **Follow up (Fu).** Have learners participate in a Twitter chat (or better yet, more than one). Ask them to identify three thought leaders to follow or find an article about your topic and share it with the rest of the industry. Many learners are using social media anyway, so why not integrate it into post-training follow-up?

- **Adult learning (Al).** Keep in mind that adult learners are autonomous beings that bring their own experiences into the learning environment. Bringing social media like Twitter into a learning program and allowing participants to research and find information can be a way of respecting that autonomy.

- **Spaced learning (Sl).** Twitter can be a helpful resource, especially for training programs that are broken up into parts. Whether you're designing a multiday or multiweek in-person course, a two-month long asynchronous online program, or a multipart e-learning course, giving an assignment in between sessions whereby learners need to research, share, or connect with others can be a way to keep your content top of mind.

- **Lesson plan (Lp).** Be intentional about the way in which you want to incorporate Twitter into your program by spelling out exactly how and when it should be used—whether in the middle of class or as a follow-up assignment. This can be easily captured through the a lesson plan.

Element 46
LinkedIn (Li)

LinkedIn is an online social media platform that was created as a way for professionals to connect and network. Here are some key properties of LinkedIn:

- Professional networking site
- Allows you to connect with anyone else who has an account (although it's most useful if you connect with those who have common professional backgrounds and goals)
- Public posts include short-form status updates, photos, videos, documents, or blog-like articles
- Interactions come in the form of commenting on someone's post, commenting in a group forum, or direct messaging those with whom you are connected
- Job opportunities may be posted or searched for

While some may see LinkedIn as "Facebook for professionals," there are many ways you can leverage this element to boost both your and your learners' abilities to grow, connect with others, and hone your craft. Here are some examples:

- **Use a private group for asynchronous online discussions.** LinkedIn allows you to create online discussion groups that are marked as "unlisted" and used to facilitate an asynchronous discussion that can take place prior to, during, or after a training session. These are easy to set up and bring the added benefit of allowing participants to connect with one another outside the formal training setting (Figure 5-2).
- **Engage in public group discussion.** There are public groups for a variety of topics, which allow you to engage with like-minded professionals or share your own information and insights. This works best when you (or your learners) approach group discussions with a sincere desire to engage in online dialogue. However, a fair criticism of

Figure 5-2. Example Unlisted Group Page on LinkedIn

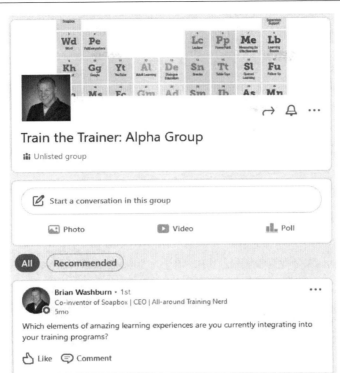

LinkedIn groups is that they're often cluttered with sales pitches and people only interested in self-promotion.

- **Establish a personal learning network (PLN), especially in the local area.** Similar to Twitter, LinkedIn allows you to connect with learning professionals across the country and around the world. With LinkedIn's more robust profiles and the ability to filter and share information, it's also an excellent way to find and connect with like-minded professionals in your local area.
- **Establish credibility in the field.** If you or your learners are seeking to establish credibility in the field, then being active on LinkedIn to share insights, articles, and resources can take you a long way. You may also choose to use LinkedIn as a blogging platform through which you can share longer form thoughts or insights. Just be sure to avoid

using phrases like "thought leader" in your description. You don't get to stick that label on yourself. Let others do that for you.

Harnessing the power of LinkedIn in an intentional way can be made easier when you apply a bond between this element and one or more of the following:

- **Adult learning (Al).** Yes, a key facet to adult learning is to respect the autonomy of the learner, but relevance is also an essential principle. LinkedIn is a big place, so if you're planning to use it as a piece of your learning program, you'll want to ensure that you clearly point to resources, links, or people that are most relevant to the experience you're trying to create.

- **Spaced learning (Sl).** As you can see from the example of setting up a private group, LinkedIn can be used to carry on asynchronous discussions during a program to keep content front-of-mind for learners. Asking learners to conduct research and find articles relevant to your topic may also be a way to leverage LinkedIn while spacing the learning out.

- **Mentorship (Mn).** LinkedIn, by its very nature, is about connecting people with similar professional interests. There may be times when it's difficult to find a mentor for an employee (or yourself) within an organization. LinkedIn makes the potential pool of mentors, at least on an informal level, much larger.

- **Goal setting (Gs).** As a platform to check once or twice a day and learn a thing or two, LinkedIn works just fine. When faced with specific goals, such as "Connect with at least five new people in the field" while attending a conference or "Find and post one new article each day," this element can give you even more power to help you improve your craft.

Element 47
Blog (Bl)

A blog, which derives from the term "web-log," is an online space that individuals (or teams or organizations) can use to publish articles and content for the world to see. There are many websites that make it easy for you to set up and host a blog, some of the most popular are WordPress, Medium, and Blogger. These are some characteristics of a blog:

- Informal, web-based writing medium that doesn't require an editor or approval to be published

- Articles may be as long or short as the writer wishes
- Primary interaction comes through reader comments in a comment section

Some organizations have an internal blog on which executives or other key leaders will share information. Some training professionals also post on internal organizational blogs or push out blog posts through their LMS. Here are three ways you may be able to take advantage of a blogging platform within the context of your next learning program:

- **Pre-session reading.** Specific blog posts that are relevant to your topic can expose learners to concepts or outside experts that can serve to prime your learners for what they'll be exploring in your training program. You can make this even more interactive by challenging learners to read and comment on a blog post or respond to another's comments in the comment section.
- **Self-directed learning.** Writing and maintaining a blog regularly— whether it's an assignment you give to participants for the duration of the learning program or it's a challenge you choose to take on yourself to hone your craft (and writing skills)—will force you to stay current on practices and trends associated with the topic of your blog. Having written and maintained a blog regularly since 2013, committing to posting two to three times per week has forced me to constantly scan the field, find fresh voices and new tools, and look for inspiration in everyday learning experiences.
- **Post-event follow-up.** Similar to the purpose of pre-work in exposing learners to outside experts and new concepts, you may wish to hold off on assigning outside blog posts until after a learning event so your learners will have a stronger foundation on which to build additional knowledge. In addition, encourage participants to capture their own reflections and learnings and contribute to the field with a guest blog post (this can also be a great marketing tool for future courses).

As you think about experimenting with incorporating blogs into your learning programs, you may consider forming a bond with the following elements:

- **Video (Vi).** While blogging is typically thought of as a written medium, sometimes it's easier to record reflections, thoughts about concepts, or reactions via video and post that on the blogging site. (This action is sometimes called vlogging.)

- **Dialogue education (De).** Blog posts may seem like digital magazine articles, but by their nature of living on the internet, blogs generally offer a forum for more back-and-forth dialogue. Often, valuable learning experiences come from the comments and discussion at the end of a post, not the blog post itself.
- **Follow up (Fu).** You may wish to be intentional and incorporate a request for participants to draft a blog post or assign a blog post to be read (and commented on) following a learning experience to keep the content fresh and front-of-mind.
- **Microlearning (Mc).** There may be times when assigning a blog post is the entire learning experience. If this is the case, make sure you send along questions for the learners to keep in mind as they read, which can help focus their attention on the most important pieces of the post.
- **YouTube (Yt).** Many blogging sites allow you to supplement your written content with an embedded link to video-sharing sites like YouTube.
- **SlideShare (Sh).** Similar to embedding a YouTube video into a blog post, you may also wish to embed a slide deck, via SlideShare, into your blog post to supplement your main points with PowerPoint-based content you have created or found to be relevant and useful.

Element 48
Website (Wb)

This might be the biggest, most generic element on the entire Periodic Table of Amazing Learning Experiences. A website, in the context of interactive elements, is a dynamic online resource that is available to anyone with an internet connection. Websites allow you to post or locate content, identify potential partners and thought leaders, and discover cutting edge tools and practices.

Why are websites considered an interactive element that can lend itself to amazing learning experiences? The answer to this important question can best be given through the following examples of ways in which a website can facilitate an environment for learning:

- **Information abounds.** Company, personal, and government sites, as well as information clearinghouses such as Wikipedia, all provide content and resources that provide a good starting point. As with any online source, you'll need to scan with a critical eye to differentiate between fact and fiction.

- **Get outside your echo chamber.** It's so easy to get lost in your own world and to think that the way your organization does things is the way everyone else does them too. It can be eye opening to see how other organizations are run (check out the About page on company websites), how they are organized (also information you can find on an About page), what drives them (how does your mission and vision compare?) and what stories they want to tell (don't just look at what information is included on the site, but also how it is presented).

Some may be asking how websites are different from element 10 (Google) or why this element isn't just named "the internet." Element 48 (website) is often used by people who aren't necessarily searching the entire internet for more information, but rather have a general (or even a specific) direction in which they need to go. For example, some jobs require heavy scanning of specific government websites to research local ordinances, find key points of contact within certain departments, or download forms that need to be submitted during a project. This type of learning need is more specific than performing a Google search and more narrow than scanning the entire body of human knowledge known as the internet.

With an element that covers such a hefty amount of information, you may want to bind it to one or more of the following elements to target your goals and outcomes:

- **Audience response (Re).** Many audience response tools are considered software as a service, run from specific websites as opposed to being installed on your local drive. This is an example of leveraging a website as a learning tool.
- **Quiz software (Qz).** Similar to audience response tools, quiz software like Kahoot or Quizizz are run from specific websites and can be fun, engaging ways to assess learners without needing to develop your own quizzing system.
- **Adult learning (Al).** Where there is a significant need for on-the-job learning, making sure employees know about key websites where they can find information, download forms, and navigate policies and procedures may be enough to honor their need to be self-directed and autonomous learners.

Element 49
YouTube (Yt)

YouTube is a video-based online social media platform that allows people to upload, share, link to, and comment on live-action content. These are core properties of YouTube:

- Content available is exclusively in video format
- The search function allows you to quickly find relevant content
- Interaction can take place by liking (thumbs up), disliking (thumbs down), sharing, or commenting on content
- Links to content can be embedded and played in blogs or websites

YouTube has been used at home and the office for on-demand learning opportunities ranging from "how do I install a new toilet" to "how do I create a pivot table in Excel." It is an excellent resource for self-directed learning, and it can be harnessed in the context of a larger, formal learning initiative. Other ways to use YouTube include:

- **Learner-generated content.** Don't feel like you need to do all the work. If you want to create an instructional video about a new policy or a video showing how to perform a certain task, your colleagues and learners may be in a better position to craft that content based upon their experiences and expertise. Devoting time during a learning experience that allows learners to create and upload content that can be shared and consumed by others across the organization (or even outside the organization) can save you time and enhance their learning experience.
- **Amplifying the reach of guest speakers or important presentations.** There may be times when key subject matter experts, top executives, or other guest speakers with limited availability are only able to work with one group of learners. Recording these presentations and making them available to those who couldn't attend the session is a way to amplify their impact.
- **Access to guest speakers.** Of course, YouTube has plenty of content from world-class speakers who are experts in just about any topic you can imagine. (Think TED Talks or similar, professionally produced conversations with high-profile speakers you otherwise wouldn't have access to at your own organization.) If you plan to use YouTube videos

in this regard to show to large or commercial audiences, just be careful about legal and copyright restrictions.

- **Brief how-to content.** Aside from world-class speakers, YouTube is full of short how-to videos you can use as part of a larger training program, as standalone microlearning pieces, or as just-in-time resources. (Just remember that these videos often range in quality and accuracy, so be sure you've done your homework on the veracity of the content created and posted by others.)

While any video content that you create can be saved to an internal drive or published to an internal file-sharing system, YouTube offers an easy-to-use platform at low or no cost, and provides the added benefit of interaction and social capabilities that your internal systems may not allow for. Of course, if you're going to use YouTube to host your content, even on a private, unlisted channel, be sure your privacy settings align with your organization's security requirements.

Bringing YouTube into a larger training program can be made more intentional and strategic by bonding it with any of the following elements:

- **Learning boosts (Lb).** Whether you use content that you've generated or credible content that you've found, sending links to YouTube videos offers an easy way to share video content while keeping your subject matter front-of-mind with your learners.
- **Video (Vi).** Obviously, this element is essential for the use of YouTube. Creating video content and posting it—whether onto a private, unlisted channel or for the whole world to see—can amplify the reach of your learning initiative by providing easy access to any audience.
- **Screen recording (Sr).** Don't think that you need to create clever, viral-caliber videos when posting to a YouTube channel. If your goal is to help people learn, then providing learning resources—whether using people or by recording screencasts and steps to navigate certain software tools—and posting them to your channel can be a crucial way to make on-demand, in-demand resources available.
- **Microlearning (Mc).** Recording or finding short clips and distributing the links to learners as stand-alone job aids or bite-sized educational chunks could be a welcome departure from articles and short e-learning modules.

Element 50
SlideShare (Sh)

You know how you send out your PowerPoint file after you've delivered a presentation? SlideShare is a social media platform that gives everyone in the world access your PowerPoint slides. Here are its core properties:

- Slide-sharing site with over 70 million users
- Allows you to upload your own content and view others' slides
- Content is easy to locate using the search function
- Interaction can come through liking, commenting, or sharing to other social media platforms

If you do plan to upload your slides to Slideshare, you *can* post them without modifying them. . . . Just like you *can* ride a bicycle without a seat, but both can be a little painful. When you distribute your slides following a presentation, most people who receive them saw your presentation and have an understanding of its context. When you share your slides via Slideshare, you're sharing your slides with the whole world, which includes a lot of people who didn't have the benefit of attending your presentation.

Making modifications to your slides so that there is some additional text on each one to explain key points you made verbally during a presentation is a good rule of thumb. For example, if I wanted to upload a slide deck from a presentation on engaging training design, I *could* upload slides that have not been modified from the way they looked during my presentation (Figure 5-3).

But is this as helpful as it could be? All you see is a slide that represents a screen capture of a really big slide deck. Perhaps with some context clues from the previous and following slides, you may understand the point I was trying to make, but why would I want you to guess?

Instead, I could spend a little time modifying my slides to make them become instantly meaningful. Does the modification in Figure 5-4, with a bar toward the bottom of the screen that explains the slide's purpose, help you better understand the point of the slide?

Remember, when someone views your slide deck on SlideShare, they will not have had the benefit of listening to your presentation, so you may need to add some explanatory text to each slide. If you're willing to put in a little work to modify and clarify some of the content on your slides,

Figure 5-3. A Slide From My Unmodified Presentation

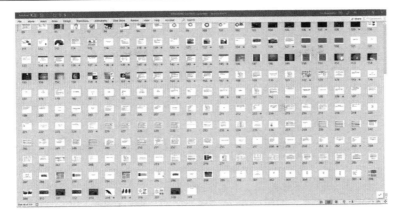

Figure 5-4. A Slide From My Modified Presentation

effectively integrating SlideShare into your training program can happen in a variety of ways:

- **Amplify your message.** As with some of the other interactive elements, SlideShare is a tool that can bring your message, concepts, ideas, and content to those outside your normal training circle—both within and outside your organization.

- **Access to good content and powerful visual design.** Many people know about using Google or YouTube to find content that others have created and bring it into their own training programs. SlideShare is a bit of a lesser-known, hidden gem that not only offers access to a lot of content from presentations others have put together, but also some strong examples of high-quality slide design. You could send out others' decks to learners like you would a blog post or a YouTube video, or they could simply serve as inspiration for how you'd like to present your own content on similar subjects.

- **Easily shareable.** Once you've uploaded your content, you can easily email the link to your slide deck to training participants without needing to worry about file-size limits. In addition, you can embed SlideShare presentations on websites or blog posts just like you would with YouTube videos.

SlideShare can be a useful way to amplify the impact of your content and can be made more powerful through bonds with any of the following elements:

- **PowerPoint (Pp).** Just like you can't leverage YouTube without videos, you obviously can't leverage SlideShare without first creating a PowerPoint deck. If you're facilitating a class on slide design, SlideShare could also be a way to encourage your participants to show you (and their peers) what they're capable of by assigning a SlideShare upload as part of the course.
- **Learning boosts (Lb).** Don't forget about the content others have already made available and posted to SlideShare. Sending links to slide decks that are aligned with your content can be a different media that helps keep your topic front-of-mind.
- **Visual design (Vd).** Just like you don't want to share poorly designed slides with your learners, you really don't want to share poorly designed slides with the rest of the world. Yes, there are some poorly designed slides that clutter up the SlideShare archives, but at the end of the day, slide decks that don't adhere to basic principles of visual design are as underwhelming on SlideShare as they are in the training environment. Be sure to not only put some effort into your visual design, but as I've shown here, also take some time to modify your slides so anyone who views them can understand the point of each one.

Element 51
Email (Em)

The final element on the periodic table is perhaps the one used most often—every day in all aspects of our lives, both personal and professional. Email is an electronic form of communication that allows people to send and receive information in the body of a message or through a file attachment. It has been commonly used and widely accessible since the early 1990s and hasn't changed much since then, except maybe that most of us now have access to email everywhere we go through our mobile devices.

If you want to experiment with this element so commonly found at home and in the office, here are a few specific ways it can be used to enhance a learning program:

- **Create a drip campaign.** Scheduling a series of emails that provide information, content, resources, surveys, and other learning instruments can be a way to transform your program from a standalone event to an ongoing learning experience. Using a tool like MailChimp lets you enter your learners' contact information and automate an entire campaign in which your learners receive messaging, information, and even assignments at a regular interval.
- **Opportunities for informal learning.** Never forget the power of informal learning when peers exchange information. While nothing can replace the magic when you visit a co-worker's cubicle in person, sometimes that's not logistically possible. Email has made the world a much smaller place, and a well-timed email to share thoughts or ideas with a colleague in a different office can lead to a quick exchange of information or a full-on brainstorming or problem-solving session.
- **Providing incentives.** Sometimes it's difficult for trainers to find out just what the learners have chosen to do with their newfound knowledge or skills once a course has been completed (think: Level 3 evaluation). It can be helpful to ask participants to email you with some examples of how they've put your content into action. In return, you can respond with a Certificate of Completion (after all, the course isn't really complete until the learner applies key learnings in real life, right?) or small giveaways like a book on the topic or even a $5 gift card for coffee.

Using email as a learning tool can work especially well when it's bonded with the following elements:

- **Supervisor support (Su).** Making sure a supervisor is included in your participant's course of learning is the best way to support the transfer of knowledge into real world application. Emailing resources—such as a course outline, goals, how it can help participants, or a goal setting template—to help make sure the right people are attending and that participants and supervisors are on the same page when it comes to value and learning outcomes can be incredibly helpful.

- **Follow up (Fu).** Once a learning program has finished, there are lots of reasons you can send an email to follow up and keep the content front-of-mind for your participant. Level 1 and Level 2 evaluations; photos of flipcharts that were taken during the session; sending resources, links, or folders from SharePoint where more information can be found; attaching the slide deck used in a class; or simply checking in to see what questions people have now that they've returned to work are all examples of ways to follow up via email.

Reflection: How Social Could Your Learning Program Be?

Is the use of one or more interactive elements appropriate for your learning program? While none of these elements are essential to the effectiveness of your program, this checklist may help you to assess areas in which certain social media platforms can heighten the level of engagement and impact of your program.

Should you use Twitter?
- ❑ Would participating in an existing Twitter chat be appropriate?
- ❑ Would it make sense to organize your own Twitter chat?
- ❑ Would you like your learners to share key points or images from your program as it's happening (live tweeting)?

Should you use LinkedIn?
- ❑ Would you like to set up an asynchronous online discussion forum?
- ❑ Would you like to publish or have learners publish longer-form writing that appears in the newsfeed of other professionals in the industry?

Should you use a blog?
- ❑ Are there experts on your topic who have published blog posts appropriate for your learners to read or comment on?
- ❑ Is there long-form information that you'd like to publish and distribute easily via a web link?

❑ Would encouraging learners to regularly reflect, constantly find new information, and publish their thoughts be an essential activity or component in a learning program?

❑ Would you like learners to publish reflections about their learning experiences in an online forum that has already been set up?

Should you use a website?

❑ Is there a specific site that learners should be visiting to research answers or download or submit forms?

❑ Would your course benefit from the creation of a microsite, developed specifically to house resources and host content from your program?

Should you use YouTube?

❑ Would video content created by those outside your organization be appropriate?

❑ Can you share video without being concerned about file size?

❑ Do you need an easy platform on which to upload learner-generated content?

Should you use SlideShare?

❑ Would slide-based content created by those outside your organization be appropriate?

❑ Would you like to distribute slide presentations without being concerned about file size?

❑ Would you like examples of how others have presented similar information?

Should you use email?

❑ Do you need to push information to a geographically dispersed audience?

❑ Would a drip campaign of ongoing content and resource delivery help with learning and retention?

Chapter 6
The X-Factor: Facilitators

We had just wrapped up a full-day train-the-trainer session and were ready to hand over the final package of training materials to our client. He was enthusiastic: "Wow, that was a really great training program. Thanks for walking us through it." But then he added, "It was great how *you* facilitated it. This program really worked well with the way *you* facilitated it, but now *I'm* going to have to facilitate it and I don't think I could ever facilitate the discussions like you did for us today."

This wasn't good. Apparently we had designed a training program with a combination of elements that would work for *me*, but we hadn't necessarily come up with a formula that would work for *the client* who would have to facilitate the training program on a regular basis.

On paper, you can have what appears to be an effective training program formula that includes research-based practices, adult learning theory, and activities proven to effectively engage learners. Of course, life isn't lived on paper, and if the initiative you're designing includes an instructor-led program, it is critical that facilitators execute the formula well in real life. Consider this formula:

$$(Lc + Rp) + (Id + Al + Gm) + Qz.$$

This program was designed to use lecture and role play with an online quizzing platform. Throughout the training session, the facilitator will adhere to appropriate instructional design, adult learning, and gamification principles. On paper, the facilitator would work with a group using this formula, leading a session that is engaging and could lead to significant change.

However, some talent development professionals—even those who have been leading training for decades—could blow this up and lead both themselves and the learners through a terrible experience. The idea of integrating an online quiz platform such as Kahoot and needing to provide instructions for, monitor, and facilitate a debrief for a role-play activity could prove too much. Whether you're designing a program for yourself or for someone else to deliver, understanding the facilitator's comfort or skill level will help you choose the right elements for the formula.

There are a variety of factors that can influence someone's comfort level and effectiveness when presenting, and we'll explore several of the most common factors in this chapter.

Is the Trainer a "Facilitator" or "Subject Matter Expert"?

A number of years ago I had the opportunity to sit with training expert Bob Pike at a conference. I asked him what he thought about using "trainer" versus "facilitator" to describe the person who delivers a training session.

Pike pulled out a piece of paper and drew a line. At one end he wrote the term *subject matter expert*. At the other end, he wrote *facilitator* (Figure 6-1). He explained that there's a continuum of people who train, and a continuum of presentation skills and abilities.

As you've read in chapter 3 about radioactive elements, a subject matter expert (element 14) is someone with significant experience, education, or expertise on a specific topic. They're not paid to design engaging training programs; they're often paid to make money for companies by putting their expertise to work. When they're asked to present on a topic, they generally share information, but pure SMEs rarely focus on engaging design. Thus, they fall at the far end of the continuum.

At the other end of this continuum is the facilitator. In its purest form, a facilitator is someone who can engage an audience in discussion and can give clear, easy to follow instructions for activities.

Then, in the middle, where some subject matter expertise is combined with some facilitation skills, falls the trainer role.

Figure 6-1. The SME–Facilitator Continuum

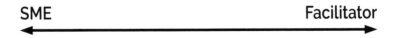

Years later, when I began to dig into this concept more to reinforce the idea that subject matter expertise is important, but facilitation abilities are just as critical, I was a little surprised by what I found in a brief scan of research.

An article in *Training Industry* put the spotlight on a small study in which 116 trainers were asked to deliver a 30-minute session on a topic of their choosing, and then were evaluated on a host of variables, including both content mastery (that is, subject matter expertise) and facilitation abilities (El Kholy 2017). Based on the overall evaluation of these trainers, one conclusion was that if trainers didn't "master the content they are delivering, that weakness could overshadow their delivery skills." Several other studies I found had similar conclusions.

Therefore, I concluded that landing somewhere to the left of center on the continuum would be the sweet spot for presenter credibility.

The SME–Facilitator continuum model isn't just something that Bob Pike and I discussed at a conference. People have been comparing the way SMEs and facilitators approach a presentation for a long, long time.

As I spent more time thinking about the concept, I began to like this two-dimensional continuum less and less. For example, where would someone like Bill Nye the Science Guy fall? He's certainly a SME in all sorts of science-related things, but he also has a very engaging, audience-centric way of focusing on teaching.

Taking a Multidimensional Look at Presentation Style and Ability

To replace the two-dimensional continuum, I've begun to use a matrix-style model to help people get a better sense for their own style, and to better calibrate training design to the style of someone else who may be asked to deliver a training program (Figure 6-2).

Figure 6-2. A Presentation Style and Ability Matrix

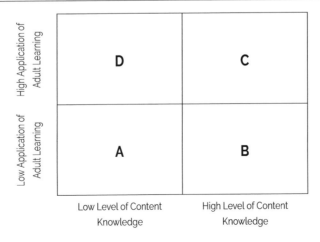

As I mentioned at the beginning of this chapter, it's important to keep both your audience and the facilitator in mind when designing learning programs.

When I first introduced the concept of a two-by-two matrix, I asked readers of our *Train Like a Champion* blog—a community comprising mainly learning and development professionals—two questions: "Which quadrant do you fall into?" and "Which quadrant do those you design for fall into?" Their answers are shown in Figure 6-3.

Figure 6-3. Designer and Presenter Aren't Always the Same Person

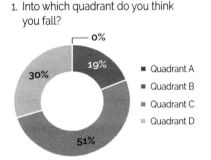

The fact that 8 percent of respondents said that they only designed training programs for themselves is a good reminder that a very large number of training initiatives are being designed for *someone else* to deliver. While it's not surprising that a survey of mostly L&D professionals netted zero people self-identifying as Quadrant A: Low Level of Content Knowledge/Low Application of Adult Learning (after all, L&D professionals ought to be applying adult learning regardless of how familiar they are with the content they're delivering), it is important to keep in mind that almost a third of respondents were designing for other people who did fall into that category.

This is why I call the facilitator of a training program the X-factor. If the program you're designing is one you could deliver easily, would that be true for others? Will anyone who picks up your training plan also be able to deliver it easily, effectively, and comfortably? If not, they'll likely cut some corners (or activities), which could change the entire outlook of the program.

Let's take a closer look at the kind of facilitator you'll find in each of these quadrants.

Quadrant A

Quadrant A consists of people who lack deep content knowledge and are unlikely to put principles of adult learning into action during their presentations. (These people are often those who have been asked or "volun-told" to present.)

When I first started using this model, someone asked: Who would ever want to be in quadrant A? Truthfully, I don't think anyone would actually want to land in this quadrant—it would probably be an extremely uncomfortable place to be. Think of this: How would you feel if you had to get up in front of people (which in itself can be uncomfortable to many), present on content that you may not be very familiar with, and you didn't know how to engage people during your presentation? Can you imagine the energy you would feel draining from your audience in this situation?

Yet many people are put into this position every day. Think about the HR generalist who is asked to lead the new employee orientation and speak to all sorts of aspects of the organization and explain the function of various teams. Or team meetings in which managers have been told to present a new policy that's been thrust upon them and to which all their team members need to adhere. Think about the colleague who is asked to fill in for a sick co-worker at the last minute.

If you know that you're designing for someone who falls into quadrant A, you can't expect the presenter to use (or even care about) adult learning theory. You'll want to make things as simple as possible, keeping content clear and straightforward while keeping activities and instructions for the participants well-written and easy to understand.

With this in mind, the following elements could prove helpful when designing for presenters in quadrant A:

- **Lecture (Lc).** Lecture is the default delivery mechanism for many people, probably because it's familiar and comfortable. While lecture may be well-suited for presenters in quadrant A because of its simplicity, it's important to not get lazy in the design process. Tightly structured notes with key talking points and examples for the presenter to follow can help make sure any lecture is focused and meaningful. Organizing lecture notes in the form of a structured story they can tell or using a "Top 10 Reasons Why [Insert Content Here] Is Important" are two ways to tightly control the lecture design while still allowing for a sense of levity.

- **PowerPoint (Pp).** PowerPoint and lecture often go hand-in-hand. People in quadrant A may not have the time or know-how to put together a deck that can visually engage their audience. Equipping a presenter with a standard set of slides helps you control the visual aspect of a presentation you've designed and makes life a little easier on the presenter.
- **Video (Vi).** When a subject matter expert cannot be physically present, it can prove helpful for those with little content mastery to have access to videos that offer a much more in-depth understanding of the subject matter.
- **Handouts (Hn).** While participants may not remember much from a presenter who falls in this quadrant, equipping them with handouts, job aids, flow charts, and resource sheets can help them revisit key points later.
- **Lesson plan (Lp).** Providing documentation on how to present information, for how long, and how to navigate any activities is a crucial step to set quadrant A presenters up for some semblance of success. A lesson plan can provide a vital road map for presenters who may otherwise be uncomfortable presenting this information.
- **Flipchart (Fc).** In a world where PowerPoint dominates the visual aspect of meetings and training sessions, the element of flipchart offers presenters an opportunity to build ideas or content dynamically. Capturing thoughts and ideas on a flipchart requires little in the way of advanced facilitation skills and can help keep participants engaged by offering a different learning medium.

While quadrant A presenters may not always need to be coddled, you should take great care if you're leaning toward integrating the following elements into a program they will be leading:

- **Quiz software (Qz).** Quiz software often needs to be set up in advance and is generally internet-based. You can help a presenter by setting up questions in the software in advance and giving detailed instructions for how to access the quiz. Including a slide for participants that clearly details how to participate in any sort of quizzing can also help mitigate confusion. Unfortunately, if there are connectivity or bandwidth issues and the presenter cannot access the quiz, it could lead to a bad experience for both a potentially panicked facilitator as well as a confused or unfulfilled group of participants.

- **Role play (Rp).** Role play is listed as a radioactive element for a reason. While clear instructions and well-crafted scenarios can help set the stage for an engaging learning experience, if the presenter isn't comfortable giving directions, monitoring small group interactions, or facilitating a dynamic debrief, participants could end up questioning the value of this type of activity.

- **Games (Ga).** One of the most challenging things about games— whether you play them in the training room or during a family game night—is a clear understanding of the directions, especially if it's a new game. It may be asking too much to expect a quadrant A facilitator to be able to help clarify instructions, monitor play, and provide in-depth insights about the subject matter covered during the training game.

Quadrant B

Quadrant B consists of those who could traditionally be labeled subject matter experts—people with high levels of content knowledge (which is why they've been hired by a company) but a low propensity to incorporate principles of adult learning in their delivery (usually because their day job is to know a lot about a topic, not about how adults learn).

I don't believe anyone *wants* to be a boring presenter. In fact, I've worked with a number of people who I'd put into quadrant B who know they're sup-posed to engage their audience. I'd put presenters into quadrant B not because they don't try to engage their audience, but because they don't, can't, or won't *apply principles of adult learning into their presentations.* Just because there is a game of *Jeopardy* or you want to make your presentation "highly interactive" by requesting that participants ask lots of questions doesn't mean you're actu-ally applying principles of adult learning.

I spent years designing in-house train-the-trainer programs in hopes that my colleagues who fell into Quadrant B would develop an appreciation for adult learning and how people retain information. To their credit, many of the SMEs I worked with did exactly that and bought into the idea that their presentations could be both informative and engaging.

Asking presenters in quadrant B to deliver highly engaging presentations, facilitate tricky conversations, and rehearse until every element of their session is perfected is probably an unreasonable request, and it's important to keep this in mind when designing for them.

When used judiciously, the following elements may prove helpful when designing for quadrant B presenters:

- **Audience response (Re).** Using audience response technology, or even simply integrating a low-tech poll by having participants raise their hands in response to a series of questions, can be an easy way to encourage presenters to engage their audience. Beware of internet-based technical difficulties with polling, though; if the presenter feels confident enough to facilitate this, they'll be rewarded not only with an engaged audience but more information about their audience and the opportunity to tailor their approach.

- **Lecture (Lc).** Many quadrant B presenters will feel most comfortable using lecture. Your challenge as a designer will be to ensure that lecture has a tight structure, a clear set of talking points, and information that answers the participant question "what's in it for me?"

- **PowerPoint (Pp).** Providing visual aids that help keep a quadrant B presenter on topic can be helpful for both presenter and participants. In addition, keep in mind that they'll probably be using PowerPoint, so if you're able to design their slides you can have control over the visual design and scope of content.

- **Video (Vi).** There may be times when a video-based animation that clearly breaks down the content or a clip of a more engaging SME (think Bill Nye the Science Guy!) can help change things up and allow participants a chance to hear from a different voice.

- **Handouts (Hn).** Always keep the forgetting curve in mind. Handouts, job aids, and other printed resources can assist in reminding participants about the content long after they have finished listening to a quadrant B presenter.

- **Lesson Plan (Lp).** A lesson plan provides quadrant B presenters with a road map to which they should adhere to engage the audience and keep the presentation focused. While quadrant B presenters may not know how to design an engaging presentation that adheres to adult learning principles, many will be open to giving such a presentation if it has been prepared for them.

- **Flipchart (Fc).** Inserting a discussion or activities in which a presenter must engage the audience (through brainstorming, gathering thoughts from previous experience, or voting on the perceived strength of certain ideas or concepts) can allow the presenter to build content dynamically and record key points on a flipchart.

- **Smile sheets (Sm).** Any time you design a training program, you'll want a variety of data points to gauge its effectiveness and success. Smile sheets can provide one data point, and if the questions are well-crafted, they can offer valuable insights about the effectiveness of both the program and the content delivery. The latter information can be helpful for quadrant B presenters if they're interested in improving their skills. Poorly crafted smile sheet questions, however, can offer misleading feedback about a presenter or program, so be sure to proceed with caution when it comes to this form of evaluation.

Of course, there are several elements you will want to be careful with if you're planning to include them in the design of a program that could be delivered by a quadrant B presenter:

- **Role play (Rp).** While role play can be a powerful tool, presenters who don't typically apply principles of adult learning in their program may have difficulty monitoring small group interactions or conducting a proper debrief, which is often where key learning happens in a role play segment.

- **Games (Ga).** Similar to role play, games can be a powerful training tool and you can learn a lot about the way in which participants are picking up key concepts through a well-designed game. However, quadrant B presenters may have difficulty fully understanding the purpose of a training game. They may also be challenged to deliver clear instructions, monitor group play, or facilitate an effective debrief.

Quadrant C

Ask anyone with an MBA and they'll tell you that the best place to be on a 2x2 matrix is in the upper right quadrant. This model, however, is very much situational.

I mentioned Bill Nye the Science Guy earlier. He'd probably fall comfortably into quadrant C. This quadrant is made up of very smart people who also deliver participant-centered presentations intended to engage their audience through the application of sound adult learning principles.

While many of us may design a lot of training content, I don't know many people who have both deep subject matter expertise and the ability to deliver a presentation by applying adult learning principles. I'm certainly not someone who would fall into this quadrant (unless we were doing a session specifically on presentation skills). Honestly, I don't want to.

I don't want to have to know the most intricate details about the various topics for which I'm asked to design training. The value I offer in my role as instructional designer is to not be a subject matter expert. Without the "curse of knowledge" (knowing a lot about a specific topic and thinking it's all important and must be learned by everyone else), I can focus my design on what's important and keep content aligned and narrowly focused on meeting learning objectives.

That said, I've met a number of SMEs who embrace the idea of incorporating adult learning principles into their delivery, and as long as they have a script or lesson plan, they're comfortable integrating elements designed to engage the audience in dialogue. If you're designing for presenters who fall into quadrant C, you may feel a bit like a kid in a candy shop. You can go crazy with your activities (aligned with learning objectives, of course) and be confident that the presenter will not only be comfortable delivering a participant-centric program, but that they will also be able to answer most (or all) of the questions participants have about the content.

The following elements—all of which may be considered a little more advanced and complex than those you may include for presenters in quadrants A and B—could amplify the impact of quadrant C presenters:

- **Dialogue education (De).** Beyond the basic principles of adult learning, Jane Vella's Dialogue Education model adds layers such as accountability (for both participant and presenter), safety, praxis, and sound relationships to the mix. It's one thing to make sure the content is relevant and engaging; it's another to work in partnership with participants and enter into a true dialogue.
- **Lesson plan (Lp).** Even if the presenter has mastered both the subject matter and delivery, having a plan to keep the program focused,

on time, and covering all of the material that needs to be covered is still essential.

- **Gamification (Gm).** While presenters in other quadrants may be able to pull off individual training games, you may have more room to weave key elements of gamification throughout a training program led by a quadrant C presenter. Beyond just points and leader boards, gamification can include things such as an overarching game narrative woven throughout, setting up a quest for participants to experience, and incentivizing cooperation to achieve a goal.

- **Assessment (As).** While quadrant A and B presenters may simply try to get through the presentation so they can return to their day job, a quadrant C presenter will often bring the skills needed to assess learners and adjust the session based upon observations. Assessment in this sense can come in the form of informal observations through activities or more formal quizzes injected throughout the program. A skilled facilitator who has subject matter expertise will be able to use these assessments to spend more time where participants may be struggling and less time in areas where they appear to grasp concepts more easily.

- **Role play (Rp).** Quadrant C presenters should be able to deliver clear instructions and monitor small group interactions, providing feedback as necessary. While these skills are important for any activity, they are extra important for role play activities. Role play is an opportunity for participants to practice what they've learned in a safe environment, but it can be derided (rightfully) by participants if the activity isn't designed, facilitated, or debriefed in a manner where aha moments can occur based on simulated conversations.

You may be looking for balance in this chapter, wondering which elements you may wish to avoid or be careful with for quadrant C presenters. However, I don't think there are any specific elements you'd need to take additional care with in this context. For example, you may not need to use as much lecture for speakers in this quadrant, but there is often a time and place for lecture to be part of a session.

Quadrant D

The final quadrant in this model, the upper left quadrant, would be the place in which "pure" facilitators are most likely to be found. When I think of the work I've done—both as an internal L&D resource as well as an external contractor asked to design programs for clients—this is where I've spent most of my time.

The subject matter expertise that presenters in this quadrant bring is a deep understanding of adult learning and the ability to facilitate conversations. These presenters, even more so than those found in quadrant C, will feel extremely comfortable facilitating discussion and debate, delivering effective activity instructions, and leading debriefing conversations that guide and deepen the learning process.

There are many elements that can be bonded with the design of programs that are delivered by quadrant D presenters, including:

- **Video (Vi).** The great thing about quadrant D presenters is that they not only know how to set up an activity and prime their learners to get the most out of what they're about to learn, they also know how to debrief content and activities. Adding video about key content takes a quadrant D presenter off the hook (to a degree) for needing to know the content. It can also provide a consistent message, which is important if the program is going to be led by multiple presenters.

- **Subject matter experts (Ex).** While a SME may not be expected to deliver any portion of a program designed for a quadrant D presenter, having them available to answer questions at some point during the session can ensure accuracy of information.

- **Handouts (Hn).** Making sure job aids, technical drawings, and other resources to which participants can refer during a session and can take with them for reference after the program has concluded will help keep the learning going.

- **Follow up (Fu).** Well-facilitated conversations can be impactful, but they can only go so far when it comes to combatting the forgetting curve. Incorporating some sort of follow up—whether giving tools to participants to engage with their supervisors or by emailing or texting additional information—can amplify the impact of high-quality training facilitation.

- **Lesson plan (Lp).** This is a common thread across any presentation style. Reigning in the X-factor that emerges—regardless of a presenter's content knowledge and ability to apply adult learning principles—by providing a structured plan for presentation delivery can help keep a session on time, on track, and on topic. Supplying key talking points can be a helpful guide for a presenter who may not be as comfortable with the content.

Since quadrant D presenters are similar to quadrant C presenters in that they will generally be more comfortable presenting and able to facilitate presentations that employ many different elements, I have again omitted a list of elements to avoid.

How Can You Mitigate the X-Factor?

Even within each quadrant, there will be a variety of skill levels, content expertise, and comfort in applying adult learning principles. In addition, differences in topics, context (for example, in-house training versus conference presentation), and audience can make a huge difference in the way the exact same training program is delivered on two different occasions.

While it's incredibly helpful to understand the type and skill level of the presenter you are designing a training program for, there are several additional ways to mitigate the unknowns for this "X-factor" of your training program.

Training-of-Trainers (TOT) Program

A training-of-trainers (TOT) program, sometimes called a train-the-trainer (TTT) program, is designed to prepare presenters for the successful delivery of a specific program. Often, a TOT program will include some background in the design of the training program and then offer participants the opportunity to practice delivering some or all of the training program while getting feedback from a master trainer or their peers.

While the basic reason for a TOT program should be straightforward, a variety of TOT participants can make it tricky to design. Some TOT programs are designed specifically for people who have a training background, who simply need to become familiar with the content and design of a new training program. Oftentimes, these are quadrant C or D presenters.

Other TOT programs, however, are designed for busy professionals who may have to deliver training as part of their job, but who do a lot of other things, too. Perhaps these are quadrant A or B presenters, but they can also fall into any quadrant. This group can be made up of salespeople, doctors, subject matter experts, department managers, or directors—anyone in an organization who counts delivering your training program as one line item in a much broader job description. If you have a two-day training program, you may be able to sequester this group for two days to walk them through it all and allow them to practice your training program. If you have a three-week training program, however, you still may only have two days to work with this group, and therein lies the trickiness in TOT design.

When I've designed a TOT course and I haven't had the time for participants to practice every section in the training program, there are several things I make sure to do to set trainers up for the maximum opportunity for success:

- **Schedule a complete review.** While you may not be able to spend three weeks (or however long your training program may be) learning how to deliver every last activity and piece of content, you can certainly block off enough time during your TOT for participants to review the entire program. This can be done by each individual, or you can break up sections and have different groups review different sections and summarize them for the larger group. However this complete review is done, be sure to leave plenty of time for questions and identify any areas you think could be tricky for either the trainer to navigate or for the training participants to grasp.

- **Expose trainers to as many different activities as possible.** If you're like me, you only have so many different kinds of activities up your sleeve. For example, I will incorporate a lot of small-group then large-group discussion and debriefing into my multi-day training programs. After a while, the content may change, but the fundamentals of facilitating that sort of activity generally remain the same. I will also sprinkle a few activities that participants will only experience once into multiday training programs, and these are the ones I need to make sure are facilitated correctly to maximize the training program's impact. Be sure that trainers are exposed to your unique activities—whether they have a chance to facilitate or at the very least experience them—at some point during your TOT.

A typical TOT agenda may include the following components:

- **Welcome and introductions.** An opportunity to provide an overview of the TOT program (goals, content, and agenda) and to allow participants to get to know the presenter and each other.

- **Adult learning and dialogue education basics.** Ensure that all program trainers have the same foundation and are aligned on the basic design philosophy that has been woven throughout the training program.
- **Scanning the curriculum for these principles.** It's not enough for trainers to appreciate adult learning principles, nor is it enough to simply hand them the training materials so they can become familiar with the sequence of content and activities. The next set of activities combines the adult learning primer with a review of all materials used in the training program—facilitator guides, participant guides, slides, and collateral materials—so that trainers have a specific eye toward how the principles of adult learning have been put into action throughout the training program.
- **Time to prepare practice facilitation and teach-backs.** Once trainers have familiarized themselves with the overall program, they'll need a heads up on which section they'll be responsible for practicing for their delivery. If they will be co-facilitating, they'll also need time to get to know their facilitation partner.
- **Practice facilitation and teach-backs with feedback.** This is the component of a TOT in which you can tell how much of an X-factor the trainers will continue to be. This is an opportunity for trainers to deliver the curriculum as if they were in front of a regular group of participants. It's also an opportunity for you and their peers to provide feedback. Using a feedback form that is targeted to constructive feedback is important for ensuring feedback remains tightly focused and useful.
- **Call to action and next steps.** The final component of a TOT program ensures that trainers have some direction for how they should be using the feedback and experience they receive. This component may also provide trainers with information for how and when they will be asked to deliver the training program with real participants.

Presentation Skills Training

A presentation skills training program differs from a TOT in that it is more general in nature (whereas a TOT program is designed to prepare trainers for a specific training program). Many of the features of a presentation skills training program will be the same or similar to those listed in the TOT program, such as:

- Welcome and introductions
- Adult learning and dialogue education basics
- Practice facilitation and feedback
- Call to action

A presentation skills training program may also offer an opportunity for participants to grow more familiar with the general training tools typically used by your organization, such as a lesson plan format or facilitator guide, slide or handout development guidelines, and general expectations for presentation facilitation and delivery. It may also include information about how adults learn and remember information and why certain design elements may appear in any training program they'll be asked to deliver.

Within the more general nature of a presentation skills training program, the practice facilitation component may include:

- An opportunity for participants to bring a section of a training program they, individually, need to deliver and on which they need practice. This may mean that 20 participants in a more general presentation skills training program are practicing facilitating a small piece of 20 different training programs.
- An opportunity to practice delivery of generic content or content from a training program in which all participants have some familiarity. The point here is not necessarily to demonstrate subject master expertise so much as it is to demonstrate the ability to effectively present in front of an audience.
- An opportunity to design and then practice something that participants develop during the presentation skills program.

On-Demand Resources

Of course, sometimes you don't have the opportunity to work with trainers and presenters in a workshop setting. Even though you may not be able to interact with them, you can still make resources available for those presenters who wish to hone their presentation craft and increase their X-factor.

Nobody wakes up and looks at themselves in the mirror and says: "I really hope I deliver a terrible presentation today." More often than not, they don't know where to look to find resources to help them become better presenters.

If you have a central repository for information at your organization (an internal wiki, SharePoint site, and so forth), then it can be helpful to trainers and presenters if you provide a combination of organizational resources (such as slide templates and lesson plan templates) and information about presentation skills (such as research on how adults learn and remember).

Here's a list of books that I like to recommend to people who want to improve their presentation delivery:

- *What's Your Formula? Combine Learning Elements for Impactful Training* by Brian Washburn (of course)
- *How to Be a Presentation God: Build, Design and Deliver Presentations That Dominate* by Scott Schwertly
- *Creative Training: A Train-the-Trainer Field Guide* by Becky Pike Pluth
- *Learning to Listen, Learning to Teach: The Power of Dialogue in Educating Adults* by Jane Vella
- *The Manager's Guide to Presentations* by Lauren Hug
- *Make It Stick: The Science of Successful Learning* by Peter C. Brown, Henry L. Roediger III, and Mark A. McDaniel
- *Evidence-Informed Learning Design: Creating Training to Improve Performance* by Mirjam Neelen and Paul A. Kirschner

Chapter 7
Finding the Right Formula

By now, you've read about 51 different elements that, when intentionally and thoughtfully strung together, can generate an effective and engaging learning experience. While the Periodic Table of Amazing Learning Experiences was never intended to be an all-inclusive list of every potential tool, theory, practice, or concept in the field of learning and development, it certainly covers a lot of ground.

"Should I use Prezi?" is a question that still comes up from time to time. While Prezi (and Keynote and Google Slides and other similar programs) is less ubiquitous and therefore represented on the periodic table by its more popular Microsoft cousin, the principles of element 6 (PowerPoint) should be used as a guiding principle for any presentation software you are most comfortable using. The same can be said for many of the other elements—Bloom's Taxonomy isn't mentioned specifically, but can be covered by element 39, learning objectives taxonomy; Kirkpatrick's Levels of Evaluation model isn't mentioned by name, but element 30, levels of evaluation, calls upon his work.

Going back to the question at hand, "Should I use Prezi?" my answer is, only if that element—no matter how cool or en vogue it may seem right now—will help improve your overall message and purpose. The key here is that no single element, by itself, can get your point or purpose across.

Training sessions begin with an idea (or an order from a supervisor) and a metaphorical empty beaker. Simply putting one element into that beaker—whether a traditional lecture or a highly interactive game (or even a unique tool such as Prezi)—won't have much impact.

Finding the right mix of elements, however, can be an elusive task. Using the same combination of elements time and time again can lead to a stale concoction. Bringing in new elements can be risky (the first several attempts may even blow up in your face), but continuing to pursue new, innovative combinations of elements is how you make breakthroughs.

Perhaps, by now, you are ready to go out into the world and begin experimenting with the formula that's right for you and your next training program. However, if you'd first like a little real-life practice putting together a variety of elements under a variety of conditions and circumstances, then this chapter is for you. What follows is an exercise in scenario planning in which you will need to come up with a formula that can help achieve the goals and objectives for eight real-life training scenarios.

As you read through each scenario you may even find a few that hit relatively close to home. Use what you've learned in this book and in your own experiences to come up with a formula that you think would work in the situation (or modify the given scenario slightly to fit one you're facing today). Jot down your thoughts (seriously, these pages want to be written upon) and then turn to the end of the chapter to compare your thoughts with the elements I actually used in the real-life situation. Maybe your ideas will be better than those I came up with. Or perhaps some of my ideas will spark some new ones for your next training program. Or maybe you'll have new discoveries inspired by some combination of your formula and my ideas.

Scenario 1
Request for a Half-Day Training Session

Background Information
We were working with an organization that connects high-net-worth individuals to nonprofit organizations for both technical and financial assistance. The client was seeking to educate its high-net-worth individuals about the make-up, function, and responsibilities of nonprofit boards.

The Request
Our client envisioned a training program that would last half a day (up to four hours) and could have anywhere from three to 30 participants. Attendance in the program would be optional, so we would need to demonstrate real value in the program before anyone would sacrifice four hours from their otherwise busy schedule.

Most attendees came from the for-profit sector and were either currently working in or retired from relatively high-ranking positions.

This training program would be delivered in-person, in local offices across the country, by staff members, volunteers, or subject matter experts who may (but probably didn't) have experience and background in training delivery. The client's initiative did not have the budget or the time to provide a train-the-trainer program.

Learning Objectives

By the end of this training program, participants will be able to:

- Compare and contrast nonprofit and for-profit board structures and functions.
- List the key responsibilities of nonprofit board members.
- Identify specific ways in which a nonprofit board can work with organizational leadership to amplify the impact of the organization and the mission.
- Identify the strengths and weaknesses of the board they've been partnered with.

The Elements

In the table below, jot down the elements you would use in this program, as well as how they would work together to serve your purpose. Then, once you're done, turn to page 202 to see what we did in this situation.

Element	How Will They Work Together?

Scenario 2
Replace Traditional Training Programs With Microlearning Bursts

Background Information

The leadership of a large, multinational organization saw the impact of the successful implementation of a microlearning initiative in another organization and thought microlearning could have a similar impact in their own organization.

The Request

Asking the training department to begin moving away from traditional classroom training or 15- to 20-minute long asynchronous e-learning modules, leadership requested the development of asynchronous microlearning modules to serve as the future of learning for the organization. These modules would be distributed using the organization's new, upgraded LMS, which had been rolled out a year earlier.

Modules could feature content provided by video, text, voiceover, or even short learning games, but they were intended to take no longer than 90 seconds to complete.

Learning Objectives

Here's an example of a microlearning module learning objective:

> By the end of this training program, participants will be able to:
>
> - Describe how the newest product fits into the company's established product line.

The Elements

In the table below, jot down the elements you would use in this program, as well as how they would work together to serve your purpose. Then, once you're done, turn to page 204 to see what we did in this situation.

Element	How Will They Work Together?

Scenario 3
Request for Developing a Computer System Training Program (in Spanish)

Background Information

A client whose mission revolved around providing microloans to women in Latin America was in the process of rolling out a new computer system to local healthcare agencies across the region that were supporting microloan clients.

The Request

Healthcare professionals—including doctors, nurses, and administrative staff—would be asked to use the new system to maintain computer-based medical records and move away from an old system of paper-based medical records. This would allow microloan clients to visit a variety of healthcare centers, all of whom would have up-to-date, networked records of the patient.

There was no training budget allocated for travel for the analysis or delivery phase of this project and no on-site trainers were available to deliver the program. Because the end-users were busy medical professionals, they would need to be able to access the training on their own schedules, when they had time available.

Learning Objectives

By the end of this training program:
- All users will be able to navigate the new electronic medical record system.
- Nurses and admin staff will be able to accurately record information in the system as patients give responses to basic screening questions.
- Doctors will be able to accurately update records while examining patients.

The Elements

In the table below, jot down the elements you would use in this program, as well as how they would work together to serve your purpose. Then, once you're done, turn to page 205 to see what we did in this situation.

Element	How Will They Work Together?

Scenario 4
Converting a Program From In-Person to Virtual

Background Information

A global health organization was searching for ways to make their multiday, in-person training course more effective and cost-efficient. Specifically, the problems they were trying to solve were twofold:

- It's very expensive to bring people together from various countries for a week-long training program.
- This training program was crucial for employees new to a specific role because it served as an orientation to all the policies and procedures they needed to master. However, the course was only offered a few times a year, meaning employees could be in the role for a year or more before attending the program.

The Request

The training department was given a mandate to convert this weeklong, in-person training program to one that was 100 percent virtual, deliverable many times each year, and accessible to employees as soon as they took on their new role, without waiting for the instructor-led elements of the course.

In addition to budget and staffing constraints, the organization was hesitant to rely too much on a series of asynchronous e-learning modules to deliver content. To keep up with the constantly changing realities of global health work, the company's organizational structure, departments, and policies were in a constant state of flux. The training department would not have the resources to constantly update lengthy e-learning modules. While Storyline-based e-learning could be one tool used in this overhaul, it would need to be limited and simple to update.

Learning Objectives

By the end of this training program, participants will be able to:

- Locate essential policies, procedures, resources, documents, and project information across the various online platforms used by the organization.
- Provide immediate and accurate information to project teams who are seeking guidance and advice for how to proceed under specific circumstances or conditions they perceive to be unique.
- Identify which team or department in the organization is responsible for handling specific questions or approving specific requests.
- Ensure project and program teams are in compliance with organizational and funder policies on how projects proceed and how money is spent.

The Elements

In the table below, jot down the elements you would use in this program, as well as how they would work together to serve your purpose. Then, once you're done, turn to page 206 to see what we did in this situation.

Element	How Will They Work Together?

Scenario 5
Develop a Customer Service Training Program for a Small IT Department

Background Information

The small IT department for an organization with offices across the US and around the world was seeking some assistance in developing a customer service training program for its IT staff. The training program could be up to one full day (about six hours of actual training, plus breaks and lunch). After the program was developed and a train-the-trainer workshop was held, this program would ultimately be delivered by the director of the IT department, who had no prior instructional design or facilitation training.

The Request

The program needed to be delivered to IT staff members located in two US-based offices, as well as several IT specialists located outside the United States. This meant that training delivery times needed to be taken into account if the program included a live, instructor-led training session.

Learning Objectives

By the end of this training program, participants will be able to:
- Quickly troubleshoot the nature of internal customer IT issues.
- Prioritize customer complaints during times of high-volume IT support requests.
- Respond to customer support requests in a timely manner using professional courtesy and offering a realistic timeline for resolution of issues.
- Open and update support requests in a timely manner through the help desk ticketing system.

The Elements

In the table below, jot down the elements you would use in this program, as well as how they would work together to serve your purpose. Then, once you're done, turn to page 208 to see what we did in this situation.

Element	How Will They Work Together?

Scenario 6
Create a Two-Day, International Learning Summit

Background Information

A global health organization based in the United States and with projects across south Asia and north Africa wanted to bring together key site leaders for a two-day learning summit.

The Request

The organization would invite some of the top surgeons in the world, high-ranking administrators, and junior managers for a series of educational sessions, hands-on lab sessions, and teambuilding activities.

While many of the surgeons and high-ranking administrators spoke English fluently, most of the junior managers did not. It was also important for summit organizers to keep in mind that many of the medical institution representatives came from hierarchical cultures in which junior managers would always publicly defer to anyone more senior, which could impact small- and large-group discussions.

Learning Objectives

By the end of this summit:

- Everyone will be able to evaluate the strength of the current organizational mission, vision, and values statements.
- Everyone will be able to align on the most important metrics to determine the impact of their programs.
- Administrators and managers will be able to determine when to coach employees for performance versus when to be directive with staff.
- Surgeons will be able to improve surgical techniques for specific procedures.

The Elements

In the table, jot down the elements you would use in this program, as well as how they would work together to serve your purpose. Then, once you're done, turn to page 210 to see what we did in this situation.

Element	How Will They Work Together?

Scenario 7
Develop a Court-Ordered Diversity Training

Background Information

As part of an EEOC settlement, a small business agreed to provide diversity training to its entire staff. While the language of the settlement was broad and the company's leadership could have fulfilled their responsibility by bringing the entire staff in for an hour-long off-the-shelf workshop, the leadership wanted this to be a meaningful experience.

The Request

Leadership asked a training manager to develop a training initiative that would help educate staff on potential blind spots that could lead to personal and organizational action items.

The staff was overwhelmingly white and the C-level was 100 percent male. In addition, the organization tended to have much more success with white customers.

Learning Objectives

By the end of this training program, participants will be able to:
- Define and give examples of white privilege in their work.
- Identify personal biases that may influence their personal or professional lives.
- Examine organizational data that may reveal a bias in the company's relationships with customers and vendors.
- Identify specific ways in which the organization could address blind spots.

The Elements

In the table below, jot down the elements you would use in this program, as well as how they would work together to serve your purpose. Then, once you're done, turn to page 211 to see what we did in this situation.

Element	How Will They Work Together?

turn to page 211

Scenario 8
Fix Cross-Departmental Communication

Background Information

The director of membership from a national member association with all employees located in a central headquarters building was alarmed when she received initial data from the organization's annual employee survey. Survey results revealed a perceived problem among employees that seemed to indicate a large majority thought there were cross-departmental communication issues and the word *silo* appeared in many narrative comments.

While this didn't come as a complete surprise—she had heard individuals make similar comments during one-on-one conversations—seeing organization-wide data was still jarring.

The Request

The director requested help from an outside firm to develop a two-part training program for her staff around basic communication and feedback skills. When analyzing the situation, the outside firm also recommended some basic organization development work to identify potential areas in which silos had formed and why that had happened.

The two-part training and organization development program would take place over two days in the summer, then a follow-up session would occur over two days in the fall.

Learning Objectives

By the end of this training program, participants will be able to:

- Map workflow processes and identify potential areas for silos and better communication.
- Use a specific model for giving feedback to peers.
- List the steps of Kotter's eight-step change management model.
- Identify areas and steps for specific changes in team communication.

The Elements

In the table below, jot down the elements you would use in this program, as well as how they would work together to serve your purpose. Then, once you're done, turn to page 213 to see what we did in this situation.

Element	How Will They Work Together?

Brief Discussion of What We Did in Each Scenario

Scenario 1
Half-Day Training Session

This scenario, like many of those outlined in this section, was based upon a real situation. Because the content revolved around nonprofit *boards*, we felt that it would be fun to use a *board game* in the first iteration of the project. We called it the *Board Board Game*. In it, participants learned about nonprofit board development by putting themselves in the shoes of a nonprofit executive director. The game would challenge participants to make decisions about how to work with a board through the various stages of the organization's life cycle, from founding to mature. Instead of simply learning about the theory involved in board selection and development, we intended for participants to experience the daily challenges faced and interactions involved between nonprofit staff and their boards.

Element	How They Worked Together
PowerPoint (Pp)	Keep facilitators and participants on the same page about content and activities. Because facilitators have a wide range of presentation skills and experience, and no train-the-trainer was offered, a standard PowerPoint deck presented a consistent visual aid that facilitators would not need to create on their own.
Dialogue Education (De)	Every participant in this program brought their own experiences in working with successful organizations. Dialogue education–inspired design allowed learning and key ideas to be shared not only by the facilitator but by a roomful of participants as well.
Subject Matter Experts (Ex)	Having access to nonprofit board experts during the design of the content offered real-life insights and credibility to an otherwise theoretical discussion.
Handouts (Hn)	This session was ultimately designed as an immersive game where a lot of content was revealed and learned based upon gameplay and choices made during the game. A set of handouts was provided with key concepts and content for those who needed a more structured, linear approach to learning. Handouts also allowed for participants to have a resource to which they could refer long after the training was completed.
Lesson Plan (Lp)	Without a train-the-trainer program, the best we could offer was a clear set of facilitator instructions in a comprehensive set of lesson plans. Like the PowerPoint deck, the lesson plans were intended to ensure consistent content and activity instructions, regardless of facilitator or geography.
Gamification (Gm)	With the subject matter focused on nonprofit board management, the use of an immersive board game could not only be a fun play on the concept of a board of directors, it could help put participants in the shoes of organizational management at various stages of organization and board development.
Smile Sheets (Sm)	To gauge participant reaction and capture highlights and key learning from a fairly unconventionally designed learning program (an immersive game instead of a typical lecture-based or more linearly-designed program).
Visual Design (Vd)	With a heavy reliance on PowerPoint slides and a game board to navigate the program, the visual experience was a significant component of the learning process. A professional graphic designer was engaged to develop visually attractive and effective program materials.

A final note about what happened in this example: As you learned in chapter 3, "Radioactive Elements," where I discussed games, the concept of the *Board Board Game* didn't go over well during the pilot phase of this project. We realized that rather than gamifying this training program—by integrating game elements throughout the whole program design—we'd simply dropped a game into the middle of the program. Given the tight turn-around between the pilot and the actual large-scale roll-out, we decided to swap out the game for a simpler activity that showcased the same content in a more straightforward way.

This experience illustrated just how crucial it is to test and pilot training programs, regardless of how well-designed they appear on paper. Being able to test and iterate—as well as willing to make major adjustments and checking your ego so you can let go of flawed designs—are the keys to delivering an effective end product.

Scenario 2
Replace Traditional Training With Microlearning Bursts

Even though the company wanted an end product that was no longer than 90 seconds, there were a lot of elements to consider to ensure learning was targeted and the microlearning modules were effective.

While leadership requested a full conversion from more traditional training delivery methods to microlearning, we worked with the training department to reframe the initiative and embrace microlearning as a useful tool while also acknowledging the role of other training delivery methods, such as instructor-led training, asynchronous e-learning programs, simple job aids, and longer-form instructional videos (among other training strategies).

Element	How They Worked Together
Video (Vi)	We were able to meet some learning objectives primarily through the use of edited existing marketing videos as a learning medium.
Adult Learning (Al)	Even short modules—or perhaps especially short modules—should adhere to key principles of adult learning to ensure that the audience can use the material to address issues they are currently facing at work.
Change Management (Cm)	The design and deployment of microlearning modules was a very different way for employees in this organization to receive and process information. In addition, leadership needed to be educated on the impact of prioritizing short microlearning bursts over other training delivery methods.
Rapid Authoring (Ra)	For those nonvideo microlearning bursts, we used a rapid authoring tool to combine content and short activities that employees could access via the LMS.
Learning Objectives Taxonomy (Lo)	It was essential that we identified specific end of module behaviors that connected to the appropriate learning objectives. With a maximum of 90 seconds, we only had time for one focused learning objective per burst—there was no room for error. If we failed here, we would create the wrong microlearning lesson.
Games (Ga)	Taking inspiration from a variety of mobile games that were popular among our children (I'm being serious), we brought inspiration and certain game mechanics into several bursts to ensure engagement and interaction while being true to the single learning objective for the learning experience.

Scenario 3

Request for Developing a Computer System Training Program (in Spanish)

While it would have been preferable to provide this new system training with an in-person instructor who could walk people through features and immediately respond to questions—especially when working with groups of learners who may not have high levels of computer proficiency—the budget, timeline, and lack of regional trainers didn't allow for this. Instead, we used Articulate Storyline to develop an e-learning program that would blend basic system navigation with real-life examples of how and when to input information while still being present for the patient in front of you. To ensure staff could access quick refreshers on how to use specific areas of the system, we also made a downloadable PDF available. Subject matter experts were instrumental not only in providing content but also region-specific Spanish vocabulary, since the course was being developed for learners who did not speak English and nobody on our team was fluent in Spanish language medical terminology.

Element	How They Worked Together
E-Learning (El)	Due to budget constraints and the need to provide access to the training program across a number of geographic regions, e-learning seemed to be the best way to distribute information quickly and consistently. It also allowed us to offer practice in the system using mocked-up screens.
Adult Learning (Al)	While there is always a temptation to simply put information on each screen of an e-learning module, we needed to make sure that busy people in a medical office would understand the relevance and be engaged throughout the program. We used slider features to simulate real-life tasks, such as adjusting patient weight on a scale, and we challenged participants to try taking information from a patient (through voiceover) while also performing other tasks because the ability to multitask is essential in a medical office.
Subject Matter Experts (Ex)	During the design phase of this project, we spent a lot of time on Skype and Zoom, meeting with people familiar with the electronic medical records system. Those conversations helped us identify the most important parts of the system to focus on during the training program.
Handouts (Hn)	While the e-learning element would serve as a tutorial to the electronic medical records system, a downloadable user manual was also created so that learners wouldn't have to go through every aspect of the e-learning program again to remember how to use one specific feature.

Scenario 3 (cont.)

Element	How They Worked Together
Assessment (As)	To determine whether learners were "getting it," we designed a number of short activities and interactions into the e-learning program. Examples included using a slider interaction to determine the weight of a patient and then record the information into a mocked-up screen in the system and taking basic patient information from a form and recording it on a different mocked-up screen in the system. Accuracy in all these interactions could be recorded in the LMS and reports generated to understand how well the participants were learning key navigation and accuracy tasks.
Rapid Authoring (Ra)	We were able to develop this e-learning program in-house by taking advantage of Articulate Storyline. It offered all the interactive features we needed without having to learn how to code.
Screen Capture (Sc)	We took advantage of screen capture software to give us clear images, allowing us to simulate the use of the actual electronic medical record system.
Visual Design (Vd)	We pulled the appropriate color pallet from the client's style guide. We also combined character packs available through the rapid authoring software with screen capture images and complementary fonts to create a visual experience intended to keep the learners engaged.

Scenario 4
Converting a Program From In-Person to Virtual

Converting from a weeklong in-person training program to one that was 100 percent virtual turned out to be a complex undertaking that involved many elements discussed in this book. There is no simple conversion table that could help us easily bring the in-person experience to a virtual format, so the entire existing program needed to be re-imagined.

After brainstorming a variety of options and discussing challenges the client might have in relying too heavily on asynchronous e-learning modules, we agreed to a formula that included perhaps the widest range of elements of any scenario found in this chapter.

What we created would primarily be a self-study program revolving around a comprehensive participant guide, which provided detailed information about all aspects of the individual's role and included interactive features, such as:

- Questions to consider at the start of each chapter to help focus the learner on the most important information they should glean from the chapter

- Discussion prompts to which learners would need to respond via an online discussion board that would be moderated by a facilitator and include responses from peers in other regions who were going through the training program at the same time
- Guidance on how to respond to text-based learning boosts, how to complete end-of-chapter e-learning modules, and how to access weekly webinars

In addition to the participant guide, moderated online discussion board, text-based learning boosts, short culminating e-learning activities to check for understanding, and weekly webinars, learners would also be paired with a mentor. This person was a more experienced employee working in the same role (ideally from their geographic region) to whom the participant could turn with questions and discuss projects and challenges.

Element	How They Worked Together
Supervisor Support (Su)	The dispersed nature of people filling this role meant that it would be difficult for them to connect with others in a similar role. A success profile and a self-assessment were to be completed by each learner and shared with their supervisor to help guide regular one-on-one conversations.
Word (Wd)	For a more professional look and feel, many graphic designers prefer to use graphic design software such as InDesign to create manuals and other printed collateral. In this project, flexibility and easy-to-update materials were the name of the game. We chose to use Microsoft Word, which would allow the organization to more easily update materials when there were policy or departmental structure changes. We sacrificed a degree of professional visual design for maximum flexibility.
Video (Vi)	A welcome video to explain the various components of the training program helped guide new learners through this training program, which would rely upon a high degree of self-study and self-accountability.
Dialogue Education (De)	With so few actual touch points between live, virtual instructor-led sessions, it was essential that any live session allowed for a two-way flow of conversation and learning. We integrated principles of dialogue education into each webinar session to ensure learners had a chance to ask questions and actively participate in discussions. This also allowed the facilitator to assess whether or not learners were "getting it."
Handouts (Hn)	The program revolved around a self-study manual that included detailed information about all aspects of the role new employees would be taking on.
Spaced Learning (Sl)	Instead of an intensive, weeklong in-person training program, the virtual program spanned seven weeks and allowed learners time to digest the information while also challenging them to recall and apply content that had been covered during previous lessons.

Scenario 4 (cont.)

Element	How They Worked Together
Lesson Plan (Lp)	With a variety of facilitators—mostly subject matter experts and more experienced staff members with little training background—we created a facilitator guide with an answer key covering all participant activities and a lesson plan for each week's webinar.
Mentorship (Mn)	Beyond the formal training program, learners were paired with more experienced staff members working in the same role so they could ask questions and discuss challenges and projects. The mentors also offered informal learning opportunities and served as a connection to new staff members who may not have been able to discuss their work with anyone else in their own country offices.
E-Learning (El)	Even though asynchronous e-learning was limited, there was still a time and place in this training program to include short, end-of-chapter culminating activities. The learners' results in these online activities were captured by the organization's LMS and reported back to the learners' supervisors to aid in the supervisor support component of this program.
Virtual Meeting (Vm)	Webinars and mentor meetings needed to take place across wide geographical regions. Virtual meeting software allowed the organization to bridge the geography and connect many learners to their learning opportunities without having to invest time or money to leave their own offices.
Text Tools (Tt)	As a way to ensure learners were grasping key concepts, learning boosts were generated via a text tool and deployed weekly so that facilitators could gather data on the accuracy of learner responses, and learners could be challenged to access information they had already learned. This was an important component of the training program as some participants had limited access to reliable internet connections but were generally able to receive SMS-based messaging. The use of the text tool to send messages to individual devices was supported by the organization.
Games (Gm)	In lieu of a standard end-of-chapter quiz, a variety of e-learning-based games were created to check for understanding while keeping things light and engaging. Games were aligned with the themes of each chapter (for example, the chapter on financial reporting revolved around a bank robbery–themed learning game).

Scenario 5
Develop a Customer Service Training Program for a Small IT Department

While early conversations involved a debate between live, instructor-led training and asynchronous e-learning, it was eventually determined that live, instructor-led training would be the way to go. The IT department director, while recognizing that delivering live training to a dispersed workforce could be a challenge, he believed the benefits of real-time conversation outweighed the convenience of an on-demand e-learning module. In addition, live, instructor-led training would allow dispersed team members to go through a common learning experience at the same time, serving as a sort of teambuilder in addition to a professional development experience.

The initial design needed to be adjusted after the train-the-trainer program because we found that the IT department director wasn't confident in his ability to facilitate a high volume of activities with loosely structured debriefing sessions. As a result, several activities were replaced with highly structured, short lectures for which talking points and discussion questions were tightly crafted.

Element	How They Worked Together
Audience Response (Re)	To engage participants at the beginning of the session and demonstrate that IT wasn't the only department that used technological solutions, this training program kicked off with a series of poll questions using a web-based audience response system that allowed participants to see one another's responses in real time, regardless of geographic location.
Lecture (Lc)	Keeping in mind that the X-factor (facilitator) for this training initiative would be the IT department director, the program was designed to best suit his comfort level and presentation style. The program included a series of activities, as well as opportunities for the presenter to discuss departmental policies, procedures, and other content through a tightly crafted and scripted series of talking points.
PowerPoint (Pp)	PowerPoint slides were developed to ensure consistent information reached participants regardless of which session they attended. Because these slides were created for the facilitator as part of the training materials package, there was a degree of quality control to the visual design and amount of content presented on each slide.
Adult Learning (Al)	Core principles of adult learning—including ensuring the program offered specific customer service models, strategies, and best practices that could be used immediately to address low customer service scores—were embedded into the program design.
Subject Matter Experts (Ex)	A variety of subject matter experts were engaged to identify best practices, specifically in IT customer service. Knowing that a SME would also be delivering the training program, we were able to cover specific activity instructions in the facilitator materials, while being confident that the course instructor would be able to answer content-related questions that weren't necessarily written down.
Lesson Plan (Lp)	A lesson plan giving specific facilitator instructions and activity directions was reviewed during the train-the-trainer program and then handed over to the IT department director so that he could deliver a consistent experience during each program offering.

Scenario 5 (cont.)

Element	How They Worked Together
Mr. Sketch Markers (Ms)	While the participants were used to a world in which technology solved many of the organization's problems, this course was also designed to include low-tech instructional methods. Placing Mr. Sketch markers at each table served as a sort of icebreaker activity (as soon as participants walked into the room and realized the markers were scented, they began to compare their favorite scents). The markers also allowed participants to own portions of the learning process by writing down their thoughts, which then turned into ad hoc session content.
Flipchart (Fc)	A number of activities involved participant brainstorming or discussion of key ideas, which were recorded on a flipchart by the facilitator.
Virtual Meeting (Vm)	Live, instructor-led sessions were offered at various times to participants across the US and around the world. While the facilitator led the sessions from the organization's headquarters, participants could join via a virtual meeting platform from any company location.
Role Play (Rp)	To ensure participants were able to apply the new customer service module as well as key concepts from the day-long course, a role-play exercise involving a variety of customer service scenarios was used to assess participant abilities.
Data (Dt)	Baseline data, including specific customer service–related questions from the organization's annual survey, were used to determine if the training program had an impact on customer service scores. In addition, the IT department's time-to-close-support-ticket metric was also monitored following the training program.

Scenario 6
Create a Two-Day, International Learning Summit

One of the biggest challenges that summit organizers faced was combatting the mental model of many participants that training was an event, not a process. While learning opportunities would be presented throughout the two-day summit, it was also important to identify potential follow-up mechanisms and ways to keep the conversation going after the event.

In addition, the summit needed to be organized in a way that allowed all attendees to have time to have large group conversations, while also carving out time for differentiated instruction that could benefit the very different skill sets and interests of attendees. For this reason, part of the summit was designed to be a wet lab for surgeons (an opportunity for them to have hands-on practice of new surgical techniques with qualified trainers offering real-time feedback), while administrative staff and managers were given time to focus on leadership development.

Element	How They Worked Together
Quiz Software (Qz)	Prior to the summit, specific information and data was collected, compiled, summarized, and distributed to all participants. To begin the summit, an online quiz using Kahoot was given to break the ice and review key data points that would be discussed throughout the two-day summit.
Dialogue Education (De)	Using the philosophy that learning happens best when participants are engaged and work in partnership with facilitators and trainers to share thoughts and add to the content, each session was designed to be a two-way conversation. Due to the hierarchical nature of their working culture, each breakout group was intentionally distributed so that participants felt comfortable being as honest as possible while contributing to the conversation.
Follow Up (Fu)	Following the summit, a WhatsApp group was set up for junior managers to form a virtual geographic bridge so they could support one another and continue conversations that were begun during the summit. Meeting organizers could monitor the interaction and seed new conversations with discussion prompts.
Smile Sheets (Sm)	To gauge participants' thoughts about the time they'd invested in the summit, information was collected about key takeaways and overall summit value. Data from these smile sheet evaluations could be combined with other summit outcomes to plan future learning events.
Collaborative File Sharing (Cf)	To facilitate information and resource sharing across sites, a wiki was set up following the summit for attendees to contribute content and locate resources that were presented during the summit.
Data (Dt)	Because one of the summit objectives revolved around key metrics, participants were asked to compare their performance against overall program goals as well as performance at other sites. Following this analysis, original goals could be revised, new goals could be set, and high performing organizations could enjoy additional credibility as they shared practices that helped them be successful.

Scenario 7
Develop a Court-Ordered Diversity Training

There is no single solution to the challenges of inequity in the workplace, and the decision was made for this workshop to focus specifically on racial and ethnic diversity. (Other areas such as gender, generational, and socio-economic diversity among leadership, staff, customers, and vendors were reserved for a later time.)

The initiative's central focus was a half-day, in-person, instructor-led training program, which all staff was required to attend. Department heads and organizational leadership were then responsible for follow up during team and all-staff meetings.

While action was the ultimate goal, the organization also needed to educate its staff on concepts such as privilege and bias before it could take some of the most necessary corrective actions. Data generated by the organization's operations provided some important baseline data points that were used to design the overall program and steer specific conversations.

Element	How They Worked Together
Supervisor Support (Su)	Supervisors and department heads were asked to submit data in advance of the session, which would be used to transform the discussions from being theoretical to focusing on real, concrete issues that were present within the company. Following the session, supervisors and department heads were asked to work with their teams to use these conversations about race, discrimination, and inequities to bring about necessary organizational changes in relationships with staff, customers, and vendors. Some data suggested that the organization was less successful when it reached out to communities of color. Questions that remained for each department to discuss included: • Why? • What should be done about it? • How would we go about making potential changes? • How would those changes affect the business?
Video (Vi)	Employees had many opportunities to explore theory and concepts around bias, privilege, and discrimination, but one of the most impactful was a clip from ABC's *Primetime* in which a hidden camera filmed a white man and a black man going through the same series of everyday tasks, but receiving different treatment.
Dialogue Education (De)	A program like this wouldn't work without incorporating highly structured dialogue between participants, following a clear set of ground rules for conversation. The principles of *safety, respect, ideas, feeling,* and *actions* were central to the program's design.
Follow Up (Fu)	It was essential that the program's action items not just be brainstormed during the session but put to use following the session. Participants completed individual action plans that were written on three-ply NCR paper with one ply being kept by participants, one ply delivered to their managers, and the final play mailed to participants 45 days following the training program. In addition, certain action items were discussed at monthly all-staff meetings following the workshop.
Levels of Evaluation (Le)	Having demographic data about customers allowed Level 4 (results/impact) evaluation to be monitored and reported on during department and all-staff meetings following the workshop.

Scenario 7 (cont.)

Element	How They Worked Together
Data (Dt)	Data was collected from each department, but the most eye opening was customer data, which revealed that the company had much lower success rates when approaching communities of color. While other data needed to be explored in much more depth (including a deep dive into secondary and tertiary performance indicators), this customer approach data seemed to speak for itself and could be discussed and addressed almost immediately.
Email (Em)	To ensure staff took the program seriously, the organization's CEO crafted an all-staff email to talk about the personal nature of this program and his hopes for actionable outcomes.

Scenario 8
Fix Cross-Departmental Communication

It's always dangerous to try to "fix" an area of the organization when training alone generally won't do much fixing. That said, this was an instance in which training could be used to help staff engage in conversations that otherwise wouldn't take place.

In the end, per the director's request, we developed a pair of two-day workshops that were separated by several months. The first two-day session revolved around analyzing annual survey data and establishing norms of communication throughout.

Then, staff were given homework to complete before the second workshop:

1. Apply the concepts and communication models discussed and observe how, when put into action, they seem to be working.

2. Read the book *Our Iceberg Is Melting: Changing and Succeeding Under Any Condition* by Holger Rathgeber and John Kotter. This would expose them to a specific model of change management.

When staff members returned for the second two-day workshop, they had an opportunity to reflect on the concepts that they had attempted to integrate into their work. Then they were asked to identify specific steps they would need to take to ultimately "fix" their communication and silo challenges, before finally setting individual goals for how to carry the discussions and action items from the workshop forward into their work.

Element	How They Worked Together
Lecture (Lc)	While there were plenty of opportunities for activities and discussion over the course of the four days that staff ultimately spent together, there were times when data or models needed to be covered. During this program, lectures almost served as a sort of "break" for participants who were otherwise involved in some intense conversations. These "lecture breaks" were used to refocus attention on the program objectives and introduce new concepts to discuss and explore in more depth through additional activities and conversations.
Dialogue Education (De)	While the overall philosophy of dialogue education and allowing participants to own the content through conversations and dialogue with one another was woven throughout this program, the principle that showed up in some of the most important moments was *praxis*. Giving participants space to engage in practice (especially in interpersonal communication and feedback) with reflection let them try out the structure of the communication models being taught in a training environment before they were asked to use those same concepts in real life.
Spaced Learning (Sl)	Having two, 2-day sessions with several months scheduled in between was an intentional design choice, which allowed staff members an opportunity to apply certain concepts and return to the second two-day session with observations and questions in hand. Building upon those initial concepts during the second two-day session also forced participants to recall what they had learned earlier.
Change Management (Cm)	Between sessions, staff were asked to read the book, *Our Iceberg Is Melting: Changing and Succeeding Under Any Condition,* so that they could discuss the changes that needed to take place in interpersonal communication and understand how difficult it would be to change organizational culture. The second two-day session began with a book club–like conversation about specific steps that needed to take place before sustainable organizational change could take hold.
Data (Dt)	Data from the annual employee survey was the catalyst for this program and served as a baseline to determine if the program would actually "fix" the situation.
Goal Setting (Gs)	While there was an initial vision for this program (fix communication and siloing), the final day of the program involved individual goal setting that, when combined with all other individuals in attendance, could lead to personal and departmental changes.

Finding *Your* Formula

Now that you've gone through a variety of scenario planning exercises in this chapter and seen how we combined solid, liquid, gas-like, radioactive, and interactive elements to solve eight different training challenges, it's time to think about your own training programs and challenges. Perhaps there's an existing program that is ripe for being refreshed. Perhaps there's a new initiative that you need to develop and roll out in the near future. It could be a simple 60-minute workshop or a comprehensive, multi-phased employee development initiative.

Take some time to reflect on a specific project so you can think through a formula that will be right for your situation, the person (or people) who will be delivering it (if there is an instructor-led component), the people who will need to be engaged and ultimately be using the information from your program, and your organization's culture.

What is the problem or challenge you're looking to address?

What data do you have to determine?
- Is this even a problem or challenge that can be partially or completely solved by training?

- Do you have a baseline to which post-training results or performance can be compared?

- How you can best distribute the training to your learners?

- Will supervisors or other supportive relationships be available? Can they be incorporated into the training program?

- What would success look like at the end of the program?

Now go through the tables below to determine the elements you can or should incorporate, and how they'll work to address the problem or challenge you're trying to solve.

When you reach the radioactive elements, you should also think about how to ensure that they won't blow up in the face of the facilitator or the participants, leaving a toxic cloud wafting over your program for generations to come.

Solid Elements	How Will They Work Together?

Liquid Elements	How Will They Work Together?

Gas-Like Elements	How Will They Work Together?

Radioactive Elements	How Will They Work Together? How Do I Keep It Safe?

Interactive Elements	How Will They Work Together?

Glossary of Elements

Some of the terms and resources found on the periodic table included in this book may mean different things to different people. This glossary serves to ensure all readers have a common understanding of how these terms and resources are being used in the context of this book.

Element Number	Element Name	Abbv.	Element Type	Definition
1	Lesson Plan	Lp	Solid	Tool used to outline the sequence and flow of activities as well as talking points for a training session. Beyond activities and talking points, this often includes bigger picture items as well, such as learning objectives and session materials.
2	Supervisor Support	Su	Liquid	A strategy of engaging a training participant's supervisor to help support the learner before and after a learning experience in an effort to ensure skill transfer to the job.
3	Word	Wd	Solid	A Microsoft word processing application.
4	Audience Response	Re	Solid	Web-based application that allows you to survey your participants in real time.
5	Lecture	Lc	Radioactive	One-way presentation delivery method in which information is given from a speaker to the rest of the audience.
6	PowerPoint	Pp	Radioactive	A Microsoft slide design application.
7	Measuring for Effectiveness	Me	Liquid	A learning program strategy in which the efficacy of a program is measured using qualitative and/or quantitative means.
8	Learning Boosts	Lb	Liquid	A learning program strategy in which learners are sent short pieces of information, activities, or quiz questions to boost retention of a particular topic or subject.
9	Quiz Software	Qz	Solid	Web-based application that allows you to ask your learners questions and track their scoring in either an individual or team format.
10	Google	Gg	Solid	One of the most commonly used internet search engines.
11	Video	Vi	Solid	Live action, animation, or screencast recordings.

Element Number	Element Name	Abbv.	Element Type	Definition
12	Adult Learning	Al	Gas-like	A theory of instruc tion that believes learners are most likely to succeed when specific criteria are met, including ensuring that the learning content is relevant, solves a problem, and, when possible, is self-driven.
13	Dialogue Education	De	Gas-like	A theory of instruction that believes learning happens best through dialogue.
14	Subject Matter Experts	Ex	Radioactive	Individuals who have a deep understanding of a specific topic.
15	Handouts	Hn	Radioactive	Print materials distributed during a learning experience.
16	Spaced Learning	Sl	Liquid	A learning program strategy in which content is revisited over a period of time (e.g., hours, days, weeks), encouraging learners to access previously introduced topics and increasing the potential for retention.
17	Follow Up	Fu	Liquid	The practice of ensuring learners have an opportunity to revisit what they have learned through post-training contact. This could include information sent by the trainer, conversations with a supervisor, peer learning groups, or communities of practice.
18	Virtual Meeting	Vm	Solid	An online platform that allows for live, instructor-led learning experiences.
19	Mr. Sketch Markers	Ms	Solid	Writing instrument characterized by unique scents, tendency to not bleed through paper, and long lifespan.
20	Flipchart	Fc	Solid	Poster-sized paper that can be prepared in advance and hung on the wall around a training room or posted on an easel and used in the moment to highlight or emphasize key learning points.
21	Gamification	Gm	Gas-like	Instructional strategy that combines intention with a coherent collection of game elements to produce an engaging learning experience connected to objectives and outcomes.
22	Change Management	Cm	Gas-like	Strategy that considers the reasons for the barriers and paths to individual and/or organizational change to ensure the highest potential for transformation.
23	Smile Sheets	Sm	Radioactive	Nickname for post-training evaluation forms that measure a participant's reaction to a learning experience.
24	Icebreakers	Ib	Radioactive	Activities designed to help participants learn more about one another, the presenter, or the topic.

Element Number	Element Name	Abbv.	Element Type	Definition
25	Assessment	As	Liquid	Instrument used to measure individual skills, knowledge gain, retention, or learning program effectiveness.
26	Mentorship	Mn	Liquid	Pairing of individuals that allows a lesser-experienced individual to gain insights into specific pathways toward success from a more-experienced individual.
27	Rapid Authoring	Ra	Solid	Software designed to allow for the easy, quick development of e-learning without the need for advanced coding skills.
28	Screen Capture	Sc	Solid	Software that allows a user to take a picture whatever is on their computer screen.
29	Screen Recording	Sr	Solid	Software that allows a user to use live-action recording to capture navigation or other movement on their computer screen.
30	Levels of Evaluation	Le	Gas-like	A variety of distinct ways to measure a training program. These include number of attendees, number of course completions, participant reaction, knowledge gain, on-the-job skill transfer, impact on a department or organization, and return on investment.
31	Visual Design	Vd	Gas-like	The practice of incorporating basic visual design concepts to ensure print and digital materials are engaging and effective.
32	E-Learning	El	Radioactive	Learning delivery method by which content and activities are available in a digital format for learners.
33	Augmented Reality	Ar	Radioactive	Combination of software and hardware that allows learners to use a device (e.g., smartphone, tablet, laptop) to scan their environment and view or interact with objects on their devices that are not physically present.
34	Coaching	Co	Liquid	Pairing of individuals in a formal relationship in which a coach will facilitate conversation through open dialogue and questions to identify and draw out answers and strategies that may lie within the coachee to achieve specific goals.
35	Microlearning	Mc	Liquid	Short, self-directed learning segments that can serve as standalone resources or as part of a larger learning program.
36	Soapbox	Sb	Solid	Online, rapid authoring tool allowing users to quickly generate a training lesson plan with a sequence and flow of activities connected to learning outcomes.

Element Number	Element Name	Abbv.	Element Type	Definition
37	Collaborative File Sharing	Cf	Solid	Central knowledge repository in which files, resources, and information can be stored and accessed by people across teams or organizations.
38	Text Tools	Tt	Solid	Software allowing learning program designers to send SMS-based messaging, information, or activities to participants before or after training programs.
39	Learning Objectives Taxonomy	Lo	Gas-like	An organizational structure given to categories of increasingly higher-level actions, skills, or behaviors that learners should be able to demonstrate by the end of a learning program.
40	Instructional Design	Id	Gas-like	A practice by which learner or organizational needs are identified, which leads to crafting, implementing, evaluating, and refining a learning solution.
41	Role Play	Rp	Radioactive	A learning activity in a practice setting in which one or more participants enact real-world conversations and behaviors based on a specific scenario and then receive feedback.
42	Games	Ga	Radioactive	A learning activity in which game elements are used to accomplish specific learning objectives.
43	Data	Dt	Radioactive	Quantitative or qualitative points of measurement, information, or statistics.
44	Goal Setting	Gs	Liquid	The practice of establishing specific plans and action items as the result of a learning experience.
45	Twitter	Tw	Interactive	Social media and microblogging platform allowing you to share information, follow colleagues or thought leaders, and conduct short-form interactions.
46	LinkedIn	Li	Interactive	Social media platform designed for professionals to connect, share industry news and information, and job announcements. It allows you to set up private groups for asynchronous conversations.
47	Blog	Bl	Interactive	Short for *weblog*; an internet site that contains a series of journal-like entries and articles that can be of varying lengths, often allowing for reader interaction through a comment section.
48	Website	Wb	Interactive	An internet page with specific information or resources that can be used as a stand-alone learning object or part of a more comprehensive learning experience.

Element Number	Element Name	Abbv.	Element Type	Definition
49	YouTube	Yt	Interactive	One of the most popular video sharing websites on the internet. It allows users to upload videos, view videos, and comment on existing content.
50	Slideshare	Sh	Interactive	Internet site serving as a repository of slide decks, allowing users to download complete decks, clip specific slides, or comment on the work of others.
51	Email	Em	Interactive	Web-based means of communication that allows users to send messages, share information and links, and attach resources.

Suggested Reading

While each chapter focusing on elements offered a brief description of the elements found on this periodic table, you may be interested in exploring some of these concepts in more depth. Following is a list of books and articles that offer more detailed information.

Gas-Like Elements

Bean, C. 2014. *The Accidental Instructional Designer: Learning Design for the Digital Age.* Alexandria, VA: ASTD Press.

Dirksen, J. 2015. *Design for How People Learn.* Indianapolis, IN: New Riders.

Duarte, N. 2011. *slide:ology: The Art and Science of Presentation Design.* Sebastapol, CA: O'Reilly Media.

Kapp, K. 2012. *The Gamification of Learning and Instruction: Game-based Methods and Strategies for Training and Education.* San Francisco, CA: Pfeiffer.

Kirkpatrick, J., and W. Kirkpatrick. 2016. *Kirkpatrick's Four Levels of Training Evaluation.* Alexandria, VA: ATD Press.

Kegan, R., and L. Lahey. 2002. *How the Way We Talk Can Change the Way We Work: Seen Languages for Transformation.* San Francisco: Jossey-Bass.

Kotter, J. 2012. *Leading Change.* Cambridge, MA: Harvard Business Review Press.

Knowles, M. 2020. *The Adult Learner: The Definitive Classic in Adult Education and Human Resource Development,* 9th ed. New York: Routledge.

McGonigal, J. 2011. *Reality is Broken: Why Games Make Us Better and How They Can Change the World.* New York: Penguin Books.

Moore, C. 2017. *Map It: The Hands-On Guide to Strategic Training Design.* Montesa Press.

Neelen, M., and P. Kirschner. 2020. *Evidence-Informed Learning Design: Creating Training to Improve Performance.* New York: Kogan-Page Limited.

Rothwell, W. 2020. *Adult Learning Basics,* 2nd ed. Alexandria, VA: ATD Press.

Vella, J. 2002. *Learning to Listen, Learning to Teach: The Power of Dialogue in Educating Adults.* San Francisco: Jossey-Bass.

Werbach, K., and D. Hunter. 2012. *For the Win: How Game Thinking Can Revolutionize Your Business.* Philadelphia: Wharton School Press.

Liquid Elements

Broad, M., and J. Newstrom. 1992. *Transfer of Training: Action-Packed Strategies to Ensure High Payoff From Training Investments.* New York: Basic Books.

Brown, P., H. Roediger III, and M. McDaniel. 2014. *Make It Stick: The Science of Successful Learning.* Cambridge, MA: Belknap Press.

Kapp, K., and R. Defelice. 2019. *Microlearning: Short and Sweet.* Alexandria, VA: ATD Press.

Radioactive Elements

Allen, M. 2016. *Michael Allen's Guide to eLearning: Building Interactive, Fun, and Effective Learning Programs for Any Company.* Hoboken, NJ: John Wiley & Sons.

Bozarth, J. 2013. *Better Than Bullet Points: Creating Engaging e-Learning with PowerPoint.* San Francisco: John Wiley & Sons.

Clark, R., and R. Mayer. 2016. *E-Learning and the Science of Instruction: Proven Guidelines for Consumers and Designers of Multimedia Learning.* Hoboken, NJ: John Wiley & Sons.

El Kholy, M. 2017. "The Trainer as SME." *Training Industry,* November 3.

Goldsmith, J. 2014. "Revisiting the Lecture." *TD Magazine,* June.

Parkinson, M. 2018. *A Trainer's Guide to Powerpoint.* Alexandria, VA: ATD Press.

Quinn, C. 2018. *Millennials, Goldfish & Other Training Misconceptions: Debunking Learning Myths and Superstitions.* Alexandria, VA: ATD Press.

Slade, T. 2020. *The eLearning Designer's Handbook: A Practical Guide to the eLearning Development Process for New eLearning Designers.*

Thalheimer, W. 2016. *Performance-focused Smile Sheets: A Radical Rethinking of a Dangerous Artform.* Work-Learning Press.

Wood, E. 2018. *E-Learning Department of One.* Alexandria, VA: ATD Press.

Solid Elements

Chen, J. 2020. *Engaging Virtual Meetings: Openers, Games and Activities for Communication, Morale and Trust.* Hoboken, NJ: John Wiley & Sons.

Laborie, K. 2015. *Interact and Engage: 50+ Activities for Virtual Training, Meetings, and Webinars.* Alexandria, VA: ATD Press.

References

Anderson, D. 2020. "Using Hotspots and Invisible Buttons in E-Learning #296."
  E-Learning Heroes, September 4. community.articulate.com/articles/using-
  hotspots-and-invisible-buttons-in-elearning.

Bajaj, G. 2012. "Conversation With Robert Gaskins: PowerPoint at 25." Indezine
  blog, February 12. (Updated February 22, 2019). blog.indezine.com/2012/08/
  powerpoint-at-25-conversation-with.html.

Bean, C. 2014. *The Accidental Instructional Designer: Learning Design for the
  Digital Age.* Alexandria, VA: ASTD Press.

El Kholy, M. 2017. "The Trainer as SME." *Training Industry,* November 3.
  trainingindustry.com/articles/strategy-alignment-and-planning/
  the-trainer-as-sme.

Goldsmith, J. 2014. "Revisiting the Lecture." *TD* Magazine, June.

Hart, J. 2020. "Top Tools for Learning 2020." toptools4learning.com.

International Telecommunication Union (ITU). 2020. "ITU-D Statistics ICT
  Statistics." Sustainable Development Goals, itu.int/en/ITU-D/Statistics/
  Pages/stat/default.aspx.

Kohn, A. 2014. "Brain Science: Overcoming the Forgetting Curve." Learning
  Solutions, April 10. learningsolutionsmag.com/articles/1400/brain-science-
  overcoming-the-forgetting-curve.

McGonigal, J. 2011. *Reality is Broken: Why Games Make Us Better and How They
  Can Change the World.* New York: Penguin.

McSpadden, K. 2015. "You Now Have a Shorter Attention Span Than a Goldfish."
  Time, May 14. time.com/3858309/attention-spans-goldfish.

Mimeo and Challenger. 2020. "State of L&D 2020." mimeo.com/state-of-ld-
  2020-report.

Thalheimer, W. 2010. "How Much Do People Forget?" A Work-Learning Research
  Document, December. worklearning.com/wp-content/uploads/2017/10/
  How-much-do-people-forget-v12-14-2010.pdf.

Thalheimer, W. 2016. *Performance-Focused Smile Sheets: A Radical Rethinking of a
  Dangerous Art Form.* Work-Learning Press.

Vella, J. 2002. *Learning to Listen, Learning to Teach: The Power of Dialogue in
  Educating Adults.* rev. ed. San Francisco: Jossey-Bass.

Washburn, B. 2020. "How to Approach Training Like a Marketer." Train Like
  a You Listen podcast, May 18. trainlikeachampion.blog/how-to-approach-
  training-like-a-marketer-podcast.

Index

Page numbers followed by *f* and *t*, respectively, refer to figures and tables.

About the Author

Brian Washburn is the co-founder and CEO of Endurance Learning, a boutique instructional design firm specializing in generating creative and unique instructor-led or e-learning programs for a client base that ranges from small nonprofit organizations to major Fortune 500 companies. He has been dabbling in the world of instructional design and corporate training for more than 20 years. It all began as a Peace Corps volunteer in Paraguay, where he discovered the joys of standing in front of a group of participants, finding ways to engage them and using flipchart to generate dynamic visual aids.

Since then, Brian has worked mostly in the nonprofit sector, leading training teams that have been charged with world-changing missions ranging from ensuring every foster child has a safe and permanent home to eliminating corneal blindness around the globe. Brian has developed and facilitated training programs in North America, South America, Europe, Asia, and Africa. Years ago, he was named a "Top Young Trainer" by *Training* magazine, and more recently served as the president of the ATD Puget Sound chapter.

Brian can be found through his *Train Like a Champion* blog and on Twitter (@flipchartguy); he's always happy to connect on LinkedIn too. He lives in Seattle, Washington, with his two children and four fish.